The fight against 'Good as' Labor men: The Australian Labor Party and the Federal Platform 1901-1910

Dr John McSwiney

KDP – AMAZON Press

TTT

https://www.timetotransform.com.au

Title: The Fight against 'good as' Labor Men: The Australian Labor Party and the Federal Platform 1901-1910 / Dr John McSwiney, author.

ISBN:9798630377432

Cover and internal design by Dr John McSwiney

Typeset in Baskerville 12/24

This book is dedicated to my father Terry and my mother Joan.

You taught me the virtues of hard work and the value of labour as something to be proud of and protected.

Love you always

John

.

CONTENTS

ACKNOWLEDGMENTS

I am not sure where I got my love of politics but I can still remember the day my father was yelling at the television when Gough Whitlam was sacked: that was interesting!

Thankyou to my parents for instilling in me the value of labour and the importance of standing up for your rights.

Thankyou to my family for loving my eccentricities and putting up with me, including my antics on election day and the ritual watching of the human psephologist Antony Green on the ABC and the theatre of him drilling into the minutia, booth by booth and seat by seat! Love it!

Thankyou to my political heroes growing up, the Hon. Bob Hawke; the Hon. Paul Keating and the Hon. John Cain. All men of vision who understood the importance of the big picture as well as representing working men and women across Australia.

Thankyou to my university professors who entertained me over many years with a myriad of stories and anecdotes and who were passionate about politics, its role in society and the greater good that could be achieved through it. The three most notable and influential were Dennis Woodward; Brian Costar and Derek Verrall. I am indebted to all of you.

Thankyou to all my friends in politics and the trade union movement who I journeyed with for many years. Always fighting the good fight and never giving up. It was great to be a part of and has provided me with countless memories and many smiles.

1 INTRODUCTION

The official platform[1] of the Federal Parliamentary Labor Party[2] has evolved in its form and scope since the party contested Australia's first federal election in March 1901. The platform has provided Labor parliamentarians and those in the wider labour movement with a broad overview of the policies that federal Labor Governments would pursue, if elected to govern.

The platform was one of the foundation stones upon which the party existed. In 1902, the Second Commonwealth Political Labour Conference adopted a pledge to the party and the platform that would be binding on all current and future candidates wishing to contest elections for and on behalf of Labor:

> I hereby pledge myself not to oppose the candidate selected by the recognised political organisation, and if elected to do my utmost to carry out the principles embodied in the Federal Labor Platform and on all questions affecting that

---

[1] The use of the term platform in this work principally refers to the federal platform of the Australian Labor Party unless otherwise stated.
[2] The use of the term Labor in this work refers to the federal Australian Labor Party unless otherwise stated.

Platform to vote as a majority of the Parliamentary Party may decide at a duly constituted Caucus meeting.[3]

The pledge has been modified over the past 120 years with the current pledge covering all members who join the party, not just those who wish to run as Labor candidates at elections.

The one constant in over 120 years of Labor membership has revolved around a commitment to pursue the stated policy planks contained in the platform. Labor members and prospective parliamentarians make the pledge in the knowledge that if elected to form a government they are pledged to uphold the platform. Of course, making a pledge and carrying it out are two entirely different concepts and in the political arena this can be highly problematical, especially for a progressive and reformist party such as Labor.

The book analyses the formation of the Federal Labor Party[4] and the role that the party played in the federal parliament in the first decade of federation. It provides a detailed overview of Labor's involvement in enacting the platform as one of the three major parties that existed in the parliament during the period. Labor only inhabited the treasury benches for two short periods: Watson in 1904 and Fisher in 1908. However, despite this fact Labor actively pursued the platform and used its numbers and influence in the parliament to support legislation related to the platform, achieving some notable successes. Labor's successes during the

---

[3] Australian Labor Party, <u>Second Commonwealth Political Labour Conference. Official Report</u>, 1902, p.4.

[4] The author notes that the term 'Labor' as it is used in this work refers to the political wing of the movement, whilst the term 'labour' refers to the industrial wing of the movement. It is acknowledged that in its formative years, the political party was spelt 'Labour' not 'Labor', however for consistency across the entire work the latter spelling of the term Labor has been used to describe the Australian Labor Party, whilst 'Labour' has retained its generic form.

period were tempered somewhat by Watson, who after attaining and losing government in 1904, actively sought out alliances with Deakin's Protectionists that threatened Labor's very independence as a viable political party. The book highlights the fact that Labor was fortunate during this period that the administrative wing of the party through its involvement in Commonwealth Conferences put a stop to alliances and forced the parliamentary wing of the party to maintain Labor's independence as a party committed to pursuing the platform and legislating for its basic constituency; the working classes. Also, it highlights the emergence of Fisher as Labor leader and Labor's development to a point where Fisher became Prime Minister in 1908 and established the foundation for Labor to win control of both the House and the Senate in the elections of 1910. It also highlights that although Labor only held government for two short periods in 1904 and 1908, it literally held the balance of power in the parliament and but for Watson's inability to seize power on Labor's behalf the party's influence during the period in enacting the platform could have been greater.

In respect of the methodological construction of this book (and the series to follow) a basic set of 'governing criteria' was developed for the work so that all Labor governments during their respective periods could be judged. For example, in what capacity did the government control the Parliament? Did the government control the Senate? Was the government confronted with judicial and constitutional impediments? And if so, what did it do to overcome these impediments? Also, what were the economic, social and political climates, both nationally and internationally in which the government ruled? The 'governing criteria' provided a workable methodology to elucidate the central argument that Labor governments did pursue and enact the platform with substantial success.

2 ALLIANCES AND AGREEMENTS

On 24 January 1900, the Inter-Colonial Conference of Labour Delegates was convened in Sydney by the New South Wales Labour executive in Sydney with representatives from Victoria, Queensland, and South Australia (Western Australia was not represented) 'for the purpose of discussing the advisableness of forming an Australian Labor Party and to frame a Federal Labor Platform.'[5]   The delegates to Conference were determined to ensure that a Federal Labor Party would have a presence on the national political stage, just as it had in the states. The Conference comprised twenty-seven representatives, of which nineteen were current Labor members of Colonial Legislatures. The delegates to the Conference shared a vision of creating a strong and vibrant national political party that would serve the interests of the labouring classes not only at the turn of the century but also for future generations of Australians. The high calibre of the delegates was reflected by the fact that in their midst were, 'two future prime ministers, four other future Federal Ministers and another six Federal parliamentarians, beside two future state premiers.'[6] The Conference unanimously supported the establishment of a Federal Labor Party to contest the first national elections, a move vital to ensure Labor representation at the national plebiscite, a point

---

[5] *Queensland Worker*, 3 February 1900.
[6] Crisp, L.F., (1955) The Australian Federal Labour Party 1901-1951. Longmans, Green and Co. Ltd, Melbourne, Australia.

taken up by Crisp who noted:

> The 1900 conference was notable for mutual forbearance and respect for the points of view of other delegations and the autonomy of the party organisations they represented. All were content with a minimum Platform made up of policies already common to most Colonial Labor Parties and with the entire absence of a Federal Party machine. The 1900 Conference appears to have set up no continuing Federal machinery at all. Though it had adopted a uniform Platform, the conduct of the 1901 Federal Election campaign was entirely a matter for the State parties. It is impossible to gauge with certainty how faithfully all Labor candidates in all states in 1901 adhered to the 1900 Federal Platform.[7]

The Conference was successful on many levels as it provided an opportunity for labour organisations and political Labor groups to seriously look at the implications and ramifications of a federal structure of government, but more importantly as far as organised labour was concerned, it provided the foundation necessary to establish a national Labor Party as part of the proposed federal model. There is little doubt that the delegates to the Conference were aware of the need to establish a Labor Party to contest federal elections, however their primary focus was levelled at that 'first election', there was very little planning for any federal election post 1901. The focus on the first federal election is evidenced by the fact that Conference did not establish any federal party machinery to organise the federal election or to provide support to the new federal party, or Labor candidates in the ensuing campaign. The party was established without any distinct operational foundations. However, despite the lack of any party machinery, Labor

---

[7] <u>ibid.</u>, p.26.

candidates were at least provided with a four-plank fighting platform. The first federal Labor Platform was not an earth-shattering manifesto, in fact it was a very modest document:

1. Electoral reform - one adult, one vote.
2. Total exclusion of coloured and other undesirable races.
3. Amendment of the Constitution providing for
    a) Initiative and Referendum for the alteration of the Constitution;
    b) Substitution of the National Referendum for the double dissolution in the settlement of deadlocks between the two Houses.
4. Old age pensions.[8]

The platform was notably silent on the issues of industrial arbitration, free trade or protection and there was no reference to any distinct military or defence policy. However, despite its shortcomings, the implication was clear, Labor had a basic election platform from which it could launch and run a national campaign.

Australia's First Federal Election

On 1 January 1901, Australia was proclaimed a federation and the new federal constitution came into effect,[9] and on 29 and 30. March 1901, Australia went to the polls and took part in the country's first national election.[10] Labor only contested twenty-six of the seventy five seats for the House of Representatives and won sixteen seats in the House and eight seats out of thirty-six in the

---

[8] ibid., p.261.

[9] Mr Edmund Barton led an interim caretaker government until he could establish the framework for federal elections to be contested.

[10] The people in New South Wales, Victoria, Western Australia and Tasmania voted on the 29th March 1901 and the people of Queensland and South Australia voted on the 30th March 1901 for the House of Representatives and the Senate. See; http://www.aec.gov.au/history/hordates.htm

Senate.[11]   In the seat of West Sydney a young Labor candidate by the name of William Morris Hughes campaigned vigorously and outlined his views on what Labor members would pursue in the new Parliament:

> I'm afraid the Federal Parliament will have very little to do with fixing the hours of Labor and levelling-up wages by means of minimum-wage Acts - that will mostly be left to the States ... Our chief plank is of course, a White Australia. There's no compromise about that ... Then there's the codification and an amendment of the Banking laws and the establishment of an Australian National Bank ... There are other things, plenty of them, but the great questions are - White Australia, Old Age pensions, a National Bank, and a Democratic Military system.[12]

Hughes campaigned on the policy issues he regarded as important, however it is a moot point as to how many Labor candidates adopted the fighting platform and espoused the four planks on the campaign trail, for in the end there was no 'national' campaign as every state political organisation ostensibly became responsible for conducting their own election efforts:

> The question of electoral organisation and the endorsement of federal candidates was to be left to the local Labor parties, and so Labor approached federation with only those organisations that already operated, that had conducted election campaigns in previous years in the various colonies.[13]

---

[11] For a description of the Labor men elected see, McMullin, 1991, op cit., pp.44-5.

[12] *Bulletin*, 16 February 1901.

[13] McKinlay. B., The ALP: A short History of the Australian Labor Party. Heinemann Publishers, Australia, 1981, p.18.

However, despite the lack of a coordinated national campaign, Labor candidates were returned from every mainland state and although Tasmania did not return a member for the House of Representatives, they did elect a Labor Senator. It should be noted that prior to the election of the Labor Senator in Tasmania there were no elected Labor politicians in that state. It is important to note that during the first federal election the Labor party did not have an elected leader and its official spokesperson was the New South Wales State Labor Leader J.S.T McGowen. McGowen contested the election for Labor but failed to be elected. In regard to Labor's efforts during the first federal election Sawer noted:

> From his [McGowen's] speeches it is plain that Labor did not expect to be more than a small group in the federal parliament, and that it proposed, as in State politics at that time, to give its support to 'measures not men' and bargain for concessions.[14]

Sawer's analysis accords with Labor's own acknowledgment of its lack of federal organisation and election strategy, but it is important to consider that if indeed this was the case, then the rise of the party in the following ten years is nothing short of miraculous.

On 8 May 1901 the inaugural meeting of the federal members took place in a basement room of Victorian Parliament House.[15] The first Caucus elected John Christian Watson as leader in the House of Representatives and Gregor McGregor as Labor leader in the Senate. Caucus then delegated key questions of Labor's platform, constitution and rules to a six-man committee[16] who reported back

---

[14] Sawer, 1956, <u>op cit</u>., p.17

[15] The Victorian Parliament was used as the home for the Federal Parliament until 1927.

[16] The members of the Committee were J.C. Watson, D. O'Keefe, J.B.Ronald, C.McDonald, H. de Largie and E.L. Batchelor.

on 20 May 1901 and outlined their recommendations for the platform, constitution and rules of the new federal party.[17]

The first platform, although limited in its scope, played a role in defining what the immediate key objectives of the party would be in the Parliament, as well as placing a definitive statement of federal Labor's goals on the public record. The respective state labour leagues and councils had not set up any national body prior to federation to oversee the transition to a federal parliamentary structure and the new parliamentarians formed a federal Caucus[18] primarily as a flow on from the practice already adopted in some of the state parliaments, especially New South Wales.[19] However, as Weller noted, the early Caucus was anything but a settled body:

> In 1901, the institution of Caucus was accepted by the federal Labor members, many of whom had had previous experience in the colonial parliaments; but the mechanics by which the party was to work and the relationship of the federal Caucus to the extra-parliamentary organisations of the movement in each of the states were far from settled when the federal Caucus including Labor members from both houses, held its first meeting in May 1901.[20]

In the first Parliament the platform provided Labor with a policy document that addressed the major issues it would pursue, however Labor shared the Parliament with Deakin's

---

[17] See Appendix 1 - Australian Labor Party Federal Platform 1901

[18] For an overview of the evolution of Federal Labor Caucus see; Weller, P. <u>Caucus Minutes 1901 - 1949. Minutes of the meetings of the Federal Parliamentary Labor Pany. Volume 1-1901-1917</u>. Melbourne University Press, 1975, pp.5-34. Also, Faulkner, 2001, <u>op cit</u>.

[19] The term 'Caucus' was already in use in New South Wales when in 1891, thirty-five Labor parliamentarians applied the term to describe their party meetings.

[20] Weller, 1975, <u>op cit</u>., p.6.

'Protectionists' and Reid's Free Traders' and although Deakin was Prime Minister, no single party held an absolute majority to govern in its own right. Labor played a minor role in proceedings which was not surprising given its numbers, however it was ever vigilant to ensure that it was heard extolling the virtues of the planks in its platform. Labor's impact during the first session of Parliament was minimal, however in the Senate, Senator McGregor left no illusions as to how Labor would use its numbers to secure platform planks stating, "We are for sale, and we will get the auctioneer when he comes, and take care that he is the right man."[21]

White Australia

Labor's biggest achievement during the session centred on its unconditional support of the Immigration Restriction Bill and the Pacific Islanders Bill in line with plank 1 of the fighting and general platform that espoused the 'Maintenance of a White Australia', with Labor's support ensuring passage of what came to be known as the 'White Australia Policy'. On 31 July 1901 Caucus officially approved the passage of the Immigration Restriction Bill stating:

> That the Party work for the total exclusion of coloured people whether British subjects or not, and to prevent importation of labour under contract.

> That the Party approves of the educational test as to coloured British subjects, with such amendments as may seem necessary; but opposes absolutely the admission of all coloured aliens.[22]

Labor's primary concern in maintaining a 'White Australia' were economic and racial. The party believed that cheap coloured

---

[21] *C.P.D.*, Vol. 1, 22 May 1901, p.763.
[22] *Caucus Minutes*, 31 July 1901.

labour should be excluded from Australian shores because the use of such labour threatened to undermine the rights and conditions of Australian workers. On 6 September 1901, Hughes outlined Labor's position on the Bill stating:

> We are to work out our destiny unaffected by that terrible blot referred to by the Attorney General as affecting America, without the leprous curse that is spreading its sway through Queensland unhampered and unhindered, and which threatens to make it a country no longer fit for a white man, because it will shortly be a country where no white man can compete with our cheap, industrious, and virtuous, but undesirable Japanese and Chinese friends. The Attorney General has said that we object to these people, because of their virtues. I do not object to their virtues, when weighed in the economic scale, become vices. For a man to work for a wage of 2d. a day is a vice which, if it became general amongst white men, would reduce society to chaos ... There is no vice, and I say it advisedly, like the vice of small expenditure when carried to a ridiculous and unEuropean length, and as this alien competition aims a blow at the very basis of our industrial system, we oppose it.[23]

Hughes was followed by Labor leader, John Watson, who not only agreed with Hughes's assertions concerning the economic perils of coloured immigration but also regarded the possible mixing of different races through marriage as the main reason why they [coloured immigrants] should be kept out of Australia:

> As far as I am concerned, the objection I have to mixing of these coloured people with the white people of Australia - although I admit it is to a large extent tinged with

---

[23] *C.P.D.*, Vol. V, 6 September 1901, p.4822.

> considerations of an industrial nature - lies in the main in the possibility and probability of racial contamination. ... The racial aspect of the question, in my opinion, is the larger and more important one; but the industrial aspect also has to be considered.[24]

The debate over white Australia and the further strengthening of plank 1 of the platform was carried over into the Pacific Island Labourers Bill which sought the exclusion of Kanaka labour from the Queensland sugar fields. On 9 October 1901 Watson outlined Labor's support for the legislation:

> I am glad that the Government have introduced this measure at a comparatively early period of the session ... The feeling that I entertain upon this question is that even if it means the absolute annihilation of the sugar industry, I am prepared to vote for the abolition of the kanakas ... The whole question is one of wages and general conditions, and if white men are offered fairly good wages, and have a reasonable prospect of steady employment, there is no doubt that in the greater portion of Queensland they will be found to do the work reliably and well ... We have to consider not only the probability of the contamination of our race, but also what work of development can be carried on by means of kanaka labour in the Northern Territory; that is to say, how many of our own people will find profitable employment ... I trust that the Bill will be passed in its present state, and that it will be declared without any possibility of misunderstanding that the people of Australia have determined that semi-slavery shall end, no matter what the consequences may be.[25]

---

[24] ibid, pp.4633-4.
[25] *C.P.D.*, Vol. V, 9 October 1901, pp.5848-53.

The Pacific Island Labourers Bill was passed in the session with Labor support and although White Australia was a significant platform plank successfully pursued by Labor it was not the only plank the party pursued during this early period. On 4 April 1902 the Government introduced the Commonwealth Franchise Bill that sought to provide the vote for all men and women over the age of 21. The Bill was in line with plank 2 of the 1901 Caucus platform that advocated 'Adult suffrage' and the extension of the franchise to Australian women. On 9 April 1902 Senator Pearce outlined Labor's support for the legislation:

> It has been said, and I think it is a truism, that we have practically reached a stage at which no debate is necessary in order to prove the justice of the claims of women to the vote. I should not have risen at this stage but for the fact that there are some honourable Senators who continue to advance the old arguments against the right of women to vote, and who are still prepared to champion the lost cause of manhood suffrage alone.[26]

At the end of August 1902 Watson held a press conference in which he reviewed Labor's activities and achievements since entering the Parliament:

> In my opinion, the Labor members have done very well, and their utterances always receive attention. Our strength is not sufficient to dominate legislation, but we total sixteen in the House of Representatives and eight in the Senate. We have worked harmoniously and have secured a fair proportion of the things that we had our eyes fixed upon when we were elected. I might particularise the legislation which deals with coloured labour and alien immigration. The enactments are not likely to prove as effective as we

---

[26] *C.P.D.*, Vol. IX, 9 April 1902, p.11492.

> desired. We fought for the total exclusion of coloured labour, and that was only lost by a few votes in the House of Representatives. Still, it was something to secure the passage of legislation which puts a bar in the way of coloured labour. We have also been successful in preventing the importation of 'contract' labour ... The present position is that the importation of labour under contract is prohibited, except in the case of expert artisans for trades which do not exist in the Commonwealth[27]

In the first session Labor had shown that although not numerically strong it would do what it could to fight for its constituency. Labor had established itself in the federal arena and consolidated its position further at the Second Commonwealth Political Labor Conference in 1902 by updating and expanding the platform and adopting a new pledge for federal members. The Conference adopted a pledge, introduced by the Executive of the Political Labor League of New South Wales, that would be binding on all candidates:

> I hereby pledge myself not to oppose the candidate selected by the recognised political organisation, and if elected to do my utmost to carry out the principles embodied in the Federal Labor Platform and on all questions affecting that Platform to vote as a majority of the Parliamentary Party may decide at a duly constituted Caucus meeting.[28]

The pledge was unequivocal in its form in relation to the platform, highlighting to federal members that if elected they were bound to do their 'utmost to carry out the principles embodied in the Federal Labor Platform. Conference then discussed the content

---

[27] *Advertiser*, Adelaide, 1 September 1902

[28] Australian Labor Party, Second Commonwealth Political Labour Conference. Official Report, 1902, p.4.

and form of the new platform. The second federal platform was more substantial than the four planks of the fighting platform of 1900 and, as Labor had performed better at the polls than expected, the 1902 Interstate Conference set about distinguishing federal Labor from Deakin's 'Protectionists' and Reid's 'Free Traders', by approving a new federal platform.[29] Labor's new platform and pledge provided members with an increased understanding of what the party stood for as well as providing them with a greater sense of purpose in respect of pursuing the platform as outlined in the pledge. The revised platform, especially in the areas of defence and industrial relations were put to the test in 1903.

Defence - Australian Owned Navy

On 2 July 1903 the Government introduced the Naval Agreement Bill into the House. The Naval Bill sought to ratify an agreement, that was passed at the Imperial Conference in 1902, between the British Government and the Australian Government that ostensibly called for a British squadron to be stationed in Australian waters, and the establishment of a Royal Naval Reserve in Australia. On 14 July Watson entered the debate on the Naval Bill to outline Labor's policy position with respect of plank 5 of the platform that specifically called for a 'Citizen Military Force and Australian Owned Navy':

> I desire to say at once that I have every sympathy with those who wish to see the development of an Australian Navy ... Unfortunately, it appears that we have in power a Government which is distinctly opposed to the idea of an Australian Navy ... They [the Government] are influenced by the theory that we, as part of the British Empire, must join forces with, and practically merge our naval defence of

---

[29] See Appendix 2 - Australian Labor Party Federal Platform 1902

the Empire. I for one do not agree with that idea.[30]

Hughes, followed the lead of Watson and highlighted the fact that a British controlled Navy for Australia would not benefit Australia in a time of crisis:

> From a national standpoint, I think that, so far as we have been able to gather, the proposed agreement is not a good one ... A local naval defence force may have deficiencies, but it is only in such a fleet that we can train the naval spirit which is inherent in the British race , and which now lacks development here for want of training, and when the day of peril comes, we must have a fleet in being ... it is the business of Australians to defend Australia. The agreement put forward, no doubt, admirable, so far as the whole interests of the Empire are concerned, but it affords no assurance of safety for this particular part of the British dominions.[31]

Labor was not successful in amending the legislation to establish an Australian owned navy, but this did not deter the party or its members from advocating Labor's position on the issue.

<u>Federal Patent Laws</u>

Also, during debate on the Naval Bill the Government introduced legislation dealing with the law relating to patents. The Patents Bill was important in that plank 9 of the General Platform called for a 'Federal Patent law, providing for simplifying and cheapening the registration of patents'. On 15 July 1903 Senator De Largie outlined Labor's acceptance of the Patents Bill:

> It is a measure which is in every way creditable to the

---

[30] *C.P.D.*, Vol. XIV, 14 July 1903, pp.2044-5.
[31] *C.P.D.*, Vol. XIV, 21 July 1903, pp.2313-20.

> Government, and which, while not of an extravagant nature, is sufficiently liberal to justify its acceptance ... No doubt some slight alterations will be necessary in Committee, but on the whole the measure is one to which we can give our approval. The present Patents laws in Australia are calculated to discourage rather than encourage, an inventor, unless he be a man of considerable means, and thus able to pay for the protection of his ideas in each State. All that, however, will be changed under this Bill.[32]

The passage of the *Patent Act* 1903, with Labor support, again showed Labor's commitment to advocate the planks of its platform when the opportunity arose in the Parliament. However, Patent legislation was far from Labor's collective mindset when the Government introduced its Defence Bill on 30 June 1903.

Defence-Australian Citizen Military Forces

The Labor platform in relation to defence was covered by plank 5 that called for a 'Citizen Military Force and Australian owned Navy'. Labor had unsuccessfully advocated an Australian owned Navy during debate on the Naval Agreement Bill and now that the focus was on 'Defence', party members turned their attention to advocating a citizen military force in line with plank 5. On 4 August Watson spoke during debate in Committee about Australia's defence requirements:

> The number of men required will depend to some extent upon the nature of the defence we decide to adopt. If we go in for a large number of fixed defences, forts, floating batteries, submarine boats, and torpedoes, involving complicated machinery, and a great deal of mechanical

---

[32] *C.P.D.*, Vol. XIV, 15 July 1903, p.2106.

knowledge on the part of the men employed, as well as familiarity with the weapons to be used, we shall require a much larger number of permanent men than we should require if we set aside those means of defence, and depend almost entirely upon our field artillery and rifle corps.[33]

On 5 August Watson spoke about the importance of establishing and maintaining a viable citizen military force:

> I think that the military training of our young men would prove an excellent thing both from the individual and the national stand point ... we need 100,000 rifles even under the present system ... In addition to the 100,000 men who would actually present themselves for drill every year, we should gradually secure a very large reserve, consisting of those who had recently undergone the course of instruction, and who would be available for any emergency that might arise. It seems to me that it is necessary to provide for something in this direction because at the present time Australia is not adequately defended.[34]

The citizen military force envisaged by Watson was primarily based on a form of conscription and Watson was quickly taken to task by Fisher over the conscription question:

> This is not a joking matter and I venture to tell the leader of the Labor party that it is not a question to be dealt with without an appeal to the electors ... I seriously protest against the proposal to compel young men to undergo continuous training for a fortnight in three consecutive years ... It is much better to give assistance to the volunteer movement, and to do all that we can for the proper training

---

[33] *C.P.D.*, Vol. XV, 4 August, p.3034.
[34] *C.P.D.*, Vol. XV, 5 August, pp.3102-3.

of those who are ready to submit themselves to military discipline, and to undergo the necessary drill.[35]

The Defence Bill highlighted divisions within Labor over the issue of conscription, with Watson and Hughes supporting the measure and Fisher vehemently opposed. Hughes even went so far as to introduce an amendment to the Bill calling for universal compulsory military training, however he withdrew it when there was little support for it. The Defence Act 1903 provided Australia with the foundation to establish its military and naval forces, the forces would be voluntary in nature and would exist alongside a small permanent force who would provide training and guidance to volunteers. Labor had again provided support for measures that enacted another plank in the platform, this time in respect of plank 5 that called for a 'Citizen military force'.

Conciliation and Arbitration

The conscription issue highlighted the divergence of opinion that existed within Labor ranks over the issue, however on industrial relations matters, Labor opinion was solid. On 28 July the Government introduced the second Conciliation and Arbitration Bill into the Parliament.[36] Labor's platform on industrial matters was contained in plank 2 of the Fighting and General platforms that called for 'Compulsory arbitration to settle industrial disputes, with provision for the exclusion of the legal profession'. On 6 August, Watson outlined Labor's approach to the legislation and in a wide-ranging speech he covered a number of policy issues important to Labor, including compulsory arbitration, exclusion of the legal profession, federal coverage for state employees and preference for unionists:

---

[35] ibid., pp.3103-5.
[36] On 5 June 1901 Mr Kingston introduced a Conciliation and Arbitration Bill into the House, however the Government withdrew the legislation.

In Australia we have had a very bitter experience with strikes ... In the absence of legislation upon industrial matters, and without trades unionism, I believe that the worker would be poorly off indeed ... [37]

... in supporting compulsory arbitration, the Labor Party are assailed by two sets of people ... We have the extreme individualist and the fearful man on the employer's side, opposed to compulsory arbitration. The Labour Party has just as many bitter, if not more bitter, opponents in the extreme reformers on its own side. Although the Labour Party as a whole throughout Australia have adopted the principle of compulsory arbitration, we find that even today there is a considerable section of extremists ... who scout any idea of handing over their liberties to any tribunal such as is contemplated by this Bill.[38]

... I am sorry that the Government has not seen fit to make some provision for the exclusion of lawyers from the [Arbitration] Court ... I recognise the need for good lawyers in the community ... but the experience in New Zealand is that the parties are able to do without lawyers, and the result is that cases have been decided at an infinitesimal cost ... I think we ought to insure, as far as practicable, the settlement of these disputes at a minimum cost.[39]

In May 1903 Victorian rail workers went on strike after the Premier (Irvine) slashed their wages and working conditions. Irvine further infuriated the wider labour movement by introducing a draconian Strike Suppression Bill to beat the workers into submission. Labor was determined to curb the excesses of

---

[37] *C.P.D.*, Vol. XV, 6 August 1903, pp.3206-7.
[38] ibid., p.3211.
[39] ibid., p.3219.

parliamentarians like Irvine and after Watson had outlined Labor's position in respect of federal jurisdiction in industrial disputes, an issue not covered in the Bill, Labor moved to protect not only the workers affected but also all workers in general. Fisher unsuccessfully moved an amendment to the Bill to ensure that public servants were covered,[40] and McDonald successfully moved a motion, with the support of Protectionist radicals to ensure coverage of railway workers.[41] However, the Government reacted to Labor's amendment by promptly 'dropping' the Bill from the legislative agenda. Labor and the labour movement were stunned by the Government's actions and they campaigned vigorously at the following election over the Government's deceit and treatment of the workers.

The Conciliation and Arbitration Bill was the last piece of legislation, related to the platform, that Labor pursued before Deakin dissolved the Parliament and called a general election for 16 December 1903. The first Parliament provided Labor with a valuable insight into what was required to pursue the platform. Labor was a bit player in the House wedged between Deakin's Protectionists and Reid's Free Traders, however Labor members were undaunted by the fact that they were only a small party in the Parliament, and on issues related to the platform they pursued them with vigour and were successful in ensuring the passage of planks relating to 'White Australia', 'adult suffrage', 'patents' and a 'citizen defence force'. Federal Labor had proven to the wider labour movement that it was capable of holding its own at a national level, the real test for the party would come at the election when the Australian people would provide their opinion on the performance of the party via the ballot box.

---

[40] *C.P.D.*, Vol. XVI, 8 September 1903, pp.4751-2.

[41] ibid., p.4785.

3. THE WORLD'S FIRST FEDERAL LABOR GOVERNMENT

On 16 December 1903 Australia went to the polls with the major issues of the campaign centring on the fiscal policy of free trade or protection and for Labor, conciliation and arbitration. On the fiscal question, Labor endorsed a policy of a fiscal truce. On the issue of protection or free trade and in respect of conciliation and arbitration, the party campaigned vigorously against the Government's withdrawal of industrial legislation in the previous Parliament.

The election result provided a great boost to Labor which saw the return of twenty- five members in the House and fourteen members in the Senate, an increase of nine and six respectively. Labor had increased its representation on the cross benches by a total of fifteen new members and this increase provided the party with a new standing and measure of authority in the Parliament. Deakin was the new Prime Minister and referred to the composition of the new parliament, in cricket parlance as like having 'three elevens' in the field,[42] where no one party was in a position to dictate terms in its own right. In fact, the composition of the House was Labor - twenty-five; Protectionists - twenty-five and Free Traders - twenty-four, with one Independent.

The first Parliament had been dominated by Deakin's

---

[42] See; La Nauze, J. A., <u>Alfred Deakin: A Biography</u>. Melbourne University Press, 1979, pp. 362-380.

Protectionists and Reid's Free Traders, however the election placed Labor in the box seat to dictate terms to their advantage. In fact, the second parliament would provide a world first: the emergence of a federal Labor government. Labor now held the balance of power in the Parliament, in the House the Government only required Labor to remain neutral, however its position was strongest in the Senate where Deakin required Labor's active support to ensure passage of its legislative program. The second Parliament provided Labor with the opportunity to use its numbers to pressure Deakin to introduce legislation in line with the platform and its numbers in the Senate provided it with an opportunity to amend legislation in line with the platform.

On 2 March 1904 the Parliament resumed with Labor supporting a large portion of Deakin's legislative program. The differences between Labor and Deakin centred on key platform policy planks related to industrial relations and defence. On the issue of arbitration, Watson argued that the federal arbitration system should cover State employees, Deakin's proposals did not include this. On the issue of defence, Watson attacked Deakin's agreement with the British government on naval defence and argued that Australia should have its own naval squadron independent of British control.

Nationalisation of Tobacco and Old Age Pensions

Labor's numbers in the Senate were immediately put to use to raise issues related to the platform, especially in relation to plank 4 of the fighting and general platforms that called for the 'Nationalisation of Monopolies'. On 17 March 1904 Senator Pearce moved a motion for the nationalisation of Tobacco in line with plank 4 of the platform as part of a plan that would have seen the revenue raised by the initiative being utilised to finance plank 3 of the platform that called for the introduction of 'Old Age Pensions':

1. That in the opinion of this Senate, in order to provide the necessary money for the payment of old age pensions and for other purposes, the Commonwealth Government should undertake the manufacture and sale of tobacco, cigars and cigarettes.

2. That the foregoing resolution be referred to the House of Representatives with a message requesting their concurrence therein.

3. That a select committee, consisting of six members of the Senate and the mover, be appointed, with power to sit and confer with a similar number of members of the House of Representatives, to inquire into and report on the best method of carrying the foregoing resolution into effect.[43]

Labor's plan for funding plank 3 of the platform was dependent upon the nationalisation of the tobacco industry and Pearce outlined the case for nationalisation and how it could be achieved in line with plank 4 of the platform:

> It is very likely that the Government will contend that we have not the power to carry out this motion; but if we have not the power now - which I do not admit - I contend that it is advisable for a Select Committee to point out how we may obtain control of the trade. There are two ways - one, by an alteration of the Constitution, and the other by asking the States Governments to give us the power. I am not at all afraid that the States Governments would refuse the request, but, on the other hand, believe that they would readily grant it, seeing that they do not, and cannot, effectively exercise such a power themselves. In many of the States, in order to pay old age pensions, it will be necessary to resort to direct taxation; this, for instance, will very probably be the case in Western Australia. I believe the

---

[43] *C.P.D.*, Vol. XVIII, 17 March 1904, p.649.

States Parliaments would willingly extend the desired power to the Commonwealth, if it were understood that the proceeds of the monopoly were to be earmarked for the payment of old age pensions. I am dealing with the question as a layman, and therefore do not presume to say whether we have the power, but the committee I suggested could take legal opinion on the subject; and if it is found that we have not the power, they could recommend the course we should adopt to secure it.[44]

On 19 May 1904 the Senate approved Labor's proposal by seventeen votes to nine and immediately proceeded to appoint the select committee.[45] The success of the motion was a victory for Labor and whilst the Senate debated the nationalisation of the Tobacco Industry, Labor again moved to exert its influence in that chamber to again pursue plank 4 of the platform.

State Owned Iron Works

On 14 April 1904 Senator De Largie moved a motion for the establishment of a federal iron works:

[The] Senate affirms the principle of iron works being established and owned by the Federal Government, for the purpose of manufacturing pig-iron, and steel from native ore, believing this would be in the best interests of Australian industry, State rights, and Commonwealth prosperity.[46]

Australia did not possess a viable iron works, however De Largie

---

[44] ibid., p.659. The history of the select committee was such that it became a Royal Commission into the industry and eventually reported by majority, that the tobacco industry should be nationalised.
[45] *C.P.D.*, Vol. XIX, 19 May 1904, pp.1296-7.
[46] *C.P.D.*, Vol. XIX, 14 April 1904, p.947.

was quick to point out that once a private firm had established itself in the market then it would operate as a monopoly on the production of iron ore and steel and it was incumbent on the federal legislature to ensure that this did not occur:

> I, though a protectionist, will consider a few times before I shall vote any assistance to an individual or private company to establish an industry which should be in the hands of the Government, for the reason that, once it was established, it would be a monopoly ... Our consumption of iron would not justify the erection of more than one modem iron works, and with only one blast furnace, too. It would not be a very big iron works which had only one blast furnace. It will be seen at a glance that a private iron works would have a monopoly of the trade in Australia.[47]

On 14 April 1904 the Senate approved Labor's motions to nationalise the tobacco industry as well as De Largie's plan to establish a Government owned federal iron works by a vote of fourteen to ten.[48] Whilst Labor pursued the platform in the Senate the manoeuvring for power in the House was constant and the fiscal barrier that had existed between the two non-Labor parties was reduced when Reid, the leader of the Free Trade group all but declared that the tariff issue was dead.

The removal of the tariff issue should have brought the non-Labor parties closer, however the issues of immigration and industrial arbitration ensured that they remained independent of one another. The polarisation on the non-Labor side over issues such as immigration and industrial arbitration benefited Labor who continued to find itself in three-sided contests where it used its numbers to influence the form and scope of legislation relating to

---

[47] ibid., p.949.
[48] ibid., p.1296.

these issues.

Conciliation and Arbitration and the World's First Labor Government

On 2 March 1904 Deakin introduced the Conciliation and Arbitration Bill into the House where debate on the Bill commenced. However, it was not until the Bill was in Committee that Labor moved amendments to bring the proposed legislation in line with the platform.

Labor had discussed its official position on the legislation with Deakin prior to its introduction, however Deakin paid no heed to Labor's concerns about implementing a Bill in line with plank 2 of Labor's platform. Deakin introduced legislation that omitted any reference to Compulsory Arbitration to settle industrial disputes and failed to make provision for the exclusion of the legal profession, the key parts of plank 2 of Labor's platform. The Bill also excluded provisions relating to preference to unionists and the application of the legislation to state government employees. On 19 April during the Committee stage of debate Fisher moved an amendment to widen the scope of the Bill to cover State government employees, by proposing to amend the meaning of the term 'industrial dispute' as outlined in section 4 of the Bill[49], as well as moving another amendment calling for the inclusion of state government employees, the effect of which (unbeknown to Fisher) would bring down the Government.[50] Deakin was unimpressed with Fisher's amendment's and viewed them as a vote of confidence in his administration:

> The amendment submitted by the honourable member has been proposed by him in a manner that is absolutely

---

[49] *C.P.D.*, Vol. XVIII, 19 April 1904, p.1043.
[50] ibid.

unexceptionable ... I have already defined exactly the Government attitude. We think that the public servants of the States and the Commonwealth should not be brought under the operation of this Bill.[51]

On 21 April Fisher addressed the Committee and outlined the rationale as to why the amendment should be supported, the corollary being that a vote for the amendment would be a vote of no confidence in Deakin's Government:

> I have no desire to traverse all the arguments which have been advanced during the course of this debate ... My own idea is that a Bill of this kind should contain no restrictions whatever. The limitation which is contained in clause 4 is one to which I particularly object ... Believing as I do in State socialism, and holding that the general welfare of the people should be our first consideration, I am bound to embrace every opportunity to advance those views ... I submit, respectfully, to the Committee, that the logical and straightforward course to adopt is to make no exemption whatever in this Bill. It is illogical to include the railway servants within its provisions, and to exclude from its operation the employees in printing offices, the wharf labourers, the dock labourers and others. Let us include the whole of them. Let us wipe away all restrictions and allow the High Court to determine whether or not our action is constitutional.[52]

Fisher's reasoning was well received in the House and in the ensuing vote Fisher was successful by thirty-eight votes to twenty-nine. The vote was decisive and on 23 April 1904 Deakin tendered his resignation as Prime Minister to the Governor General. Labor

---

[51] ibid., pp.1045-1057.
[52] *C.P.D.*, Vol. XIX, 21 April 1904, pp.1242-3.

wasted little time, after Deakin's resignation, holding two special Caucus meetings; the first (in the morning) provided Watson with an opportunity to discuss the consequences of the resignation and the second (in the afternoon) provided Watson with the opportunity to inform his parliamentary colleagues that, '... [he] had waited on the Governor General and accepted the commission to form an administration.'[53]   Watsons acceptance of the commission to become Prime Minister placed Labor in a position, that four years earlier seemed impossible even to its most ardent supporters, it had achieved a place in history as the world's first national Labor government and was now in a position to pursue the platform as the legitimate government of the country.

The elevation of Labor to power did not sit well with the more conservative elements of the press who were quick to pass judgement on the new administration, with the Daily Telegraph commenting:

> They have everything to learn and nobody in the Cabinet able to teach them. It is wholly and solely an apprentice government ... It remains, however, to be seen how the curious political freak will be looked upon by the House, which need not submit to be made ridiculous one moment longer than it has a mind to.[54]

Labor now governed in the House without any support from Deakin or the old Free Traders, and according to Sawer, "Watson took office without any specific promise of support from the Protectionists as a party, though he had assurances of general 'benevolent neutrality'[55] at least from the radical high protectionist wing of that party and probably Deakin himself."[56]   Labor held

---

[53] *Caucus Minutes*, April 23, 1904
[54] *Daily Telegraph*, 27 April 1904 (lead article)
[55] Sawer, 1956, <u>op cit</u>., p.38.

office in a minority capacity, a situation that was not lost on the Argus, who smugly editorialised:

> The Ministry is of course, entitled to a fair and reasonable chance of showing what, as a minority, it can do ... It [the Government] will exist entirely on sufferance, since it has no command of the confidence of a majority; and unless it can perform the Parliamentary miracle of proving that a Ministry so situated can do good and necessary work, it has no claim to an extended life. We should regard as a public calamity the accession to power of a socialistic Government with a strong following. But the temerity of a socialistic band which composes the smallest section of the House, fortified by practically no experience of public or private business, in assuming office, can do little harm, and will probably result in much good. If such a Ministry attempts any revolutionary measures, either of administration or legislation, it will be blocked by the majority which watches it. If it shirks its platform utterances, and merely struggles feebly along on lines of compromise already laid down, it will not justify its existence. There is little to be feared from it, and all that can be hoped is that it will fill an interregnum, during which that large body of moderate and experienced men in the House ... can come together on honourable lines to form a strong party which will yield steady allegiance to a stable Government.[57]

Labor's minority status was also tested by Labor members who sought to establish a coalition with Deakin, believing that a coalition would better protect Labor's hold on power. Whilst the discussions over a coalition took place, Watson outlined Labor's

---

[56] See *C.P.D* Vol. XIX, 21 April 1904, pp.1248-1250, especially Deakin's assurances of fair play.
[57] *Argus*, 25 April 1904.

legislative plans for the following parliamentary session in line with the platform stating:

> ... [that the] Navigation Bill will be the first measure introduced, and the Old-Age Pensions Bill will be next. We admit that there are huge difficulties in the way of the establishment of a commonwealth system of old-age pensions, but difficulties are created only to be surmounted, and we think that in this case they can be surmounted ... We also propose during the next session to take steps in regard to the tobacco monopoly.[58]

On 17 May Caucus met to discuss the question of a coalition and decided that, "This Party considers it is due to its position in Parliament and its standing with the electors of the Commonwealth that its policy should be untrammelled by any coalition."[59]

The proposal for Labor to form a coalition with Deakin was defeated, however Caucus approved a proposal to support Opposition members who supported the Labor Government, "This Party will welcome the support of those members outside its ranks who elect to assist the present Ministry, or in the event of the Government being defeated support the Party when in opposition."[60] The proposal would have effectively precluded Labor from standing candidates against non-Labor incumbents in seats that Labor had an excellent opportunity of winning. The backlash to the proposal from the State branches to the proposal that had responsibility for electing candidates was quick and harsh. All states except South Australia refused to accept the proposal and this was later ratified by the Third Commonwealth Political

---

[58] McMullin, 2004, op cit., p.80.

[59] The motion was carried by 21 votes to 8; see *Caucus Minutes*, May 17, 1904.

[60] *Caucus Minutes*, May 17, 1904.

Labour Conference of 1905 as well as at the New South Wales and Victorian State Conferences. However, despite trenchant opposition from the State organisations, Caucus approved a motion to initiate a formal dialogue with Deakin.[61] As a result of the motion[62] Watson wrote to Deakin outlining his proposals for an Alliance:

> I have been empowered by the Labor Party, at a meeting held today, to enter into negotiations with you in reference to arranging an Alliance by which the Liberal and Labour Parties may be consolidated, sufficiently, at least, to ensure a program of progressive legislation being put through parliament in the immediate future.
>
> Our party recognised the desirability of securing settled administration if it can be obtained without sacrifice of principle upon the part of those concerned. Having this in view, I would suggest the following as a basis:
>
> 1. No definite arrangement to be arrived at until after the projected attack on the government has been disposed of, preferably after a vote has been taken on the inclusion of public servants in the Arbitration Bill.
> 2. In the event of an Alliance being arranged, representation in the cabinet to be accorded your party on a numerical basis, the Labor Party stipulating for a negative voice as to the individuals to be included.
> 3. Ministers and supporters to accept program for this session announced by the government.

---

[61] The Chairman made a statement with reference to a proposed alliance with certain other members and Carpenter moved that he be empowered to negotiate towards an alliance. *Caucus Minutes*, May 25, 1904.

[62] The motion was carried by a vote of 24 to 8. See *Caucus Minutes*, May 26, 1904.

Note: the railway vote will have been decided.

4. Details of next session's program to be submitted to joint party, with right of either section of joint party to withdraw from Alliance if agreement impossible.
5. All questions relating to program and conduct of affairs by ministry to go before joint party.
6. Members of joint party to be supported at elections, after the manner usual in all parties, during the continuance of the Alliance.

Trusting you may be able to submit this suggestion to your party.[63]

Watson's letter provided a workable framework on which to lay the foundation for an Alliance, although parts of the letter would have caused some angst among those in the party who believed that providing protection to non-Labor members was anathema to the advancement of Labor's ideology and platform. The Alliance proposal approved by Caucus became irrelevant as Deakin and the Liberal Protectionists were not interested, with Deakin replying, "At a meeting of the Liberal-Protectionist Party today it was resolved that present circumstances do not render advisable either of the proposed Alliances or coalitions."[64]

With no support from Deakin for an Alliance, Watson proceeded to govern in his own right. Deakin would not support Labor and his attitude to the new administration was more than matched by other Opposition members. According to McMullin, the sight of Labor Ministers occupying the Treasury benches reduced Forrest to apoplexy, with Forrest shouting out in the House, "Mr Speaker,

---

[63] Papers of Alfred Deakin, National Library of Australia, Canberra. Watson to Deakin, 26 May 1904, MS 1540-16-62-s2-v. The letter was also copied into the ALP, Caucus Minutes, Book by Frank Tudor on 1 June 1904.

[64] Papers of Alfred Deakin, National Library of Australia, Canberra. Watson to Deakin, 30 May 1904, MS 1540-16-70-s1-e.

what are these men doing in or places? Those are our seats."[65] Forrest survived this harrowing ordeal and Watson started where he had left off on 21 April by reintroducing the Conciliation and Arbitration Bill back into the Parliament.

Conciliation and Arbitration

On 31 May 1904 Watson resumed debate on the Bill moving a new amendment to the definition of 'industrial dispute' that included a clear reference to state railways employees, "That the words 'including disputes in relation to employment upon State railways' be inserted after the word 'State'."[66]

Watson's amendment becoming the first time that a Labor government (anywhere in the world) was pursuing its stated Platform goals and was definitely a cause for celebration, however, debate on the Bill was complex and drawn out and Labor spent the next three months attempting to pass the legislation through the House in the face of numerous Opposition amendments. Minority government was proving to be extremely difficult and frustrating for Watson who prophetically told Higgins that, 'I despair of seeing any good come out of this Parliament.'[67] Watson's analysis of his government's ability to successfully pursue the platform was correct and on 10 August 1904 the Opposition with some deft parliament manoeuvring and political chicanery moved an innocuous amendment to the Bill[68], the effect of which provided it with the numbers in the chamber to have the amendment passed, the corollary again being that the passage of the amendment would also be a vote of confidence in the Government. Watson and Labor

---

[65] McMullin, 1991, op cit., p.51.

[66] *C.P.D.*, Vol. XIX, 31 May 1904, p.1676.

[67] Palmer, N., Henry Bourne Higgins. Harrap Publishers, London, 1931, p.177.

[68] McCay, Deakin Protectionist, moved, 'That clause 48 be omitted from the clauses proposed to be recommitted'. See: *C.P.D.*, Vol. XXI, I 1 August 1904, p.4155.

knew the Government was in trouble and during the debate on the motion to recommit, Labor members attacked the duplicitous and underhanded way in which the Opposition had literally brought the Government to its knees. King O'Malley was the most colourful of the Labor speakers as he left no-one guessing as to how he felt about the situation:

> As a party we are game to die tonight. There is no hesitation on our part. For the three months during which I have been sitting on this side of the House I have felt like a muzzled Rocky Mountain tiger cat ... The action of the Opposition might be all right, viewed from the stand point of the Tammany Hall bludgers or the sand baggers of Pennsylvania or the Louisiana Kluklux clans, but it is altogether out of place in a British Legislature ... I had hoped that there would be no political trickery or dodgery in this Parliament, but we now have presented to us a sorrowful and pathetic sight ... The essence of democratic government consists in the preservation of human rights and no scheming or trickery should be indulged in which would endanger those rights.[69]

Deakin's political chicanery was effective and on 12 August 1904 the House divided on the motion to recommit and the amendment was passed by thirty-six votes to thirty-four. Watson immediately adjourned the session and a week later on 17 August he resigned his Government's commission and informed the House:

> I desire to intimate to the House that, following on the vote, which was given on Friday last, I waited upon His Excellency the Governor General, and offered certain advice [that the Parliament be dissolved] upon which His Excellency did not see fit to act. I then tendered the

---

[69] <u>ibid.</u>, p.4179.

> resignations of myself and colleagues, which His Excellency
> was pleased to accept..[70]

Labor's time in office was brief and although not a success in either its tenure or on its legislative achievements, it surpassed all expectations as it became the first Federal Labor Government to hold office in the world. Commenting some years later on the time during that first government, Hughes stated:

> The days passed and the business of Parliament and of the
> country went smoothly on, every day finding us more adept
> in handling the affairs of State, more nonchalant in our
> replies to questions designed to disturb our peace of mind.[71]

Watson resigned as Prime Minister and George Reid was summoned to form a Free Trade and Protectionist Coalition Government, with Allan McLean leading the Protectionist group.[72] The Reid/McLean ministry survived until the close of the session on 15 December 1904, but not before Labor and a group of radical Protectionists led by Lyne and Isaacs entered into an agreement to unseat the Reid/McLean coalition,[73] despite the earlier negative reaction of the state branches and supporters to such agreements taking place.

Labor and Alliances

Labor had shown the world that it was not only capable of governing in its own right, but that it would responsibly pursue its platform despite trenchant criticism to the contrary. However,

---

[70] *C.P.D.*, Vol. XXI, 17 August 1904, p.4264.

[71] Fitzhardinge, L., <u>William Morris Hughes Volume 1: That fiery little particle 1862 -1914.</u> Angus and Robertson, Sydney, 1964, p.163.

[72] Deakin had played a role in negotiations between the two groups but refused to join along with the radical wing of the Protectionists; see *C.P.D.*, Vol. XXV, 29 June 1905, p.60.

[73] *C.P.D.*, Vol. XXI, 7 September 1904, p.4343.

instead of focusing on making Deakin's new government accountable and pursuing the platform via negotiation and support, Labor literally became a faction of Deakin's Protectionists. On 7 September 1904 a draft proposal was agreed to and a week later on 14 September Official Articles of Alliance were ratified by Labor and the Isaacs Protectionist group. Minor amendments were made to the draft Articles but the ratified Articles of Alliance contained five general conditions of Alliance together with a seventeen part platform.[74] The adoption of the Alliance by Labor was a clear breach of the pledge and an unequivocal abandonment of Labor's official platform, for Deakin and the Protectionists policy agenda.

A majority of Labor members were positive about the Alliance believing that it presented the best possible means to extract concessions from Deakin and the Protectionists on a quid pro quo basis, even though they were aware that there was a wide legislative gulf between the Articles of Alliance and Labor's platform they had pledged to uphold. Also, the pursuit of articles two, three and four of the Alliance placed them in direct conflict with the respective state administrations. Despite the negative impact on the party, the forming of an Alliance during this period is not surprising given the political machinations of the time, however what is remarkable is that the Articles agreed to were even ratified by Caucus in the first instance. Crisp regarded Labor's foray into an Alliance as being due in large part to the, "... intolerable immediate frustrations and pressures being suffered by FPLP members under the three-party conditions of those early Parliaments."[75]

There is little doubt that Labor members felt varying degrees of

---

[74] See Appendix 3 -Articles of Alliance between the ALP and Deakin's Protectionists
[75] Crisp, 1955, <u>op cit</u>., p.160.

'frustration and pressure', however the cauldron that is the federal parliament, especially in its formative years would have had the same effect on nearly all members, not just Labor. The Conditions of the Alliance posited five express terms to be adhered to by members of both Labor and the Protectionists with respect to protecting sitting members at elections. Articles two, three and four of the Alliance were similar in substance and form to the coalition proposals of the previous May that effectively granted immunity to non-Labor sitting members at elections. The immunity provisions had already been vehemently opposed by nearly every state Labor administration as untenable, and yet only four months after the coalition proposals were soundly defeated, Labor was advocating them again and incorporating them into a formal Alliance.

Labor was aware of the ambit and potential impact of Articles two, three and four and it is arguable that they were included on the sole basis of the parliamentary party taking the initiative to manage their own affairs without the interference of the state branches. In 1904 the administrative structure of the federal party was embryonic at best and this may have been an audacious claim on the part of the parliamentary wing to establish itself as a separate entity with sole responsibility for the federal arena with the state bodies being responsible for their respective states. Placing any conjecture on the 'Conditions of Alliance' to one side, it is pertinent to also look at the Alliance agreed to by Labor and to contrast and compare it with Labor's 1902 Federal Platform that Labor members had pledged to uphold. A comparative analysis of the platform contained in the Alliance and the official platform of the party shows the deliberate omission of key planks of established Labor policy for short-term political goals that were not realisable. In fact, a closer analysis of the Articles of Alliance shows that there was very little to be gained by Labor entering an Alliance. The White Australia policy was operational, debate on the Conciliation and Arbitration Bill continued, and would soon become law, Labor

Senators were using their numbers in the Senate to initiate motions to pursue plank 4 of the platform dealing with the nationalisation of monopolies, and despite this fact Labor continued to pursue an Alliance that was not in their political interests and set them on a direct collision course with their respective State organisations.

Caucus had ratified an Alliance that effectively bound the party to the General Platform of that Alliance. In doing so Labor committed themselves to abandon planks 4 and 6 of the Labor's Fighting Platform, together with planks 7(d) & (e) and 8 and 9 respectively of the General Platform.[76] Labor's Alliance had shown that it was willing to barter with planks in the platform, planks they were pledged to uphold and planks already agreed to by the wider Labour movement. The Alliance was driven by Watson's mistaken belief that the party needed an 'Alliance' to maintain legitimacy. The Alliance by Labor was the first time that Labor had officially shown that the platform could be compromised for questionable short-term political gain, a gain that in itself was based on a spurious set of facts. Caucus (by a majority) entered into an Alliance with key planks of the party's fighting and general platforms not even cited. In fact, the abandoned planks were not even a part of the Draft Alliance considered earlier by Labor. If Labor had incorporated the entire platform into the draft proposals for discussion one could argue that at least an attempt was made to protect and advance Labor's policy planks. However, the fact that major policy initiatives were not included, even at the plenary stages of the Alliance is remarkable. It appears that Labor was willing to forego advancing major planks of the platform for a very limited and restricted opportunity to be in a position of power.

The behaviour of Labor during this period was disconcerting to the wider labour movement as it sent the signal that Labor did not

---

[76] See Appendix 2 for an overview of the abandoned Labor Party planks.

respect the platform a point made in previous Argus articles. Also, the establishment of Old Age Pensions was the third plank of Labor's Fighting and General Platforms, it was a plank in the original Platform of 1901, however Old Age Pensions were not even included in the draft proposals for an Alliance primarily because the radical protectionist Isaacs 'preferred to leave it off'. At the end of negotiations between the parties Old Age Pensions were incorporated into the Articles of Alliance as plank 15. The establishment of Old Age Pensions were deemed, in effect, of less importance than the Trade Marks Bill (plank 4); the Fraudulent Marks Bill (plank 5); the High Commissioner Bill (plank 6); the Electoral Act Amendment Bill (plank 7); the Papua Bill (plank 8); the Anti-Trust Legislation (plank 9); the Tobacco Monopoly (plank 10); the Iron Bonus Bill (plank 11) and the establishment of a Standing Committee on trade, commerce and agriculture (plank 12).

It should be noted that not one of the planks mentioned above are contained in Labor's official Fighting or General Platforms of 1902. Labor showed their collective political naivety by giving themselves no room to manoeuvre on already established Labor planks such as the Nationalisation of Monopolies; the establishment of a Citizen Military Force and Australian owned Navy; placing restrictions on public borrowing; the introduction of navigation laws to provide for the proper supply of life saving and other equipment and for the regulation of hours and conditions of work for workers, the vast majority of which were union members; the establishment of a Commonwealth Bank of Deposit and Issue, and Life and Fire Insurance Department; as well as introducing a Federal Patent Law that would simplify and cheapen the registration of patents.

The abandoned planks were not part of the official Alliance agreement, however plank 17 of the General Platform of the

Articles of Alliance provided a general clause that granted, 'either party and opportunity to submit any other subject for consideration with a view to Joint action.'[77] This clause could be considered as the 'get out' clause for Labor, a clause that it could use to introduce its omitted planks. However, it is arguable that given the political climate of the time, the Alliance would have revolved around the established core planks already included in the official Alliance agreement. The inclusion of any other 'abandoned' planks, via plank 17, would have had the distinct possibility of blowing the Alliance to pieces thus further negating any chance for Labor to extract concessions on stated platform policy.

The existence of the Alliance did not deter the Reid/McLean Government and it survived until the end of the parliamentary session on 15 December 1904. Parliament did not reassemble until 28 June 1905, however in the recess period both Labor and the Protectionist radicals had again entered into negotiations to unseat the Reid/McLean coalition. A week before the resumption of the second Parliament on 22 June 1905 Watson wrote to Deakin confidentially encouraging him to remove Reid:

> It has been suggested to me that you might be willing to undertake the direction of affairs yourself and assume office again at the head of a Government. If such an idea is in your mind, you can rely on our active support, and I think our people would prefer that to joining in a coalition. We, and especially myself, do not want office, but I have the utmost desire to stop the retrogressive movement which Reid is heading, and I feel the moment has arrived when you could take command with every prospect of success ... I feel that many moderate people who are a little afraid of us

---

[77] *Caucus Minutes*, September 6 1904.

> would rally to your support if given an opportunity ... I hope you will not hastily decide to miss the opportunity of course, a two-party position is desirable, but the Labor Party would become practically identical with the Protectionists, and that would be something gained. Of course, this letter is confidential, but I know the feeling I express is shared by a majority of the party, and they would be all glad of seeing you in the leading position again.[78]

Watson and Deakin discussed the possibility of Watson committing Labor into a coalition without incurring the wrath of the state organisations at the Third Interstate Labor Conference to be held in early July. On 28 June 1905 Parliament resumed and Prime Minister Reid pushed for a dissolution of Parliament almost immediately, however the Governor General dismissed Reid's request and instead granted Deakin his second ministry. Watson had written Deakin a note in the afternoon of the 28th stating, 'Could I see you before you leave this evening.'[79] Watson and Deakin then held discussions concerning Reid's move for a dissolution, the outcome being that Watson promised Deakin two important concessions:

1. a cordial and generous support for this parliament;[80] and
2. a pledge of cooperation in both Houses.[81]

The concessions granted by Watson were important to Deakin again becoming Prime Minister. In Deakin's previous government he purportedly only knew of Labor's intentions 'from day to day', but with Watson's concessions the Governor General was satisfied of the bona fides of Deakin's claim, however this was not before

---

[78] Papers of Alfred Deakin, National Library of Australia, Canberra. Watson to Deakin, 22 June 1905, MS 1540-16-392-s4-v.

[79] Papers of Alfred Deakin, National Library of Australia, Canberra. Watson to Deakin, 28 June 1905, MS 1540-16-420-v.

[80] La Nauze, J.A., Alfred Deakin. MUP, Melbourne, 1965, p.391.

[81] ibid., p.398.

Caucus voted down a proposal to establish a coalition government with Labor members holding four Cabinet positions stating that:

> Our allies be consulted with a view to the Constitution of a Cabinet consisting of four Labor men and three members from amongst those who support the Labor Party in ousting the present Ministry.[82]

Watson's deal with Deakin assured that Labor would never form a government in its own right and Watson appeared content to accept the fact that Deakin would not offer his support for Labor to form government. Watson was willing to prostitute himself and the platform for a few morsels from Deakin and the Protectionists table and this was nowhere more evident when on 5 July 1905 Deakin wrote to Watson outlining his Government's program for the coming Parliament, in which Deakin's proposed program was almost a carbon copy of the old Alliance agreement of September 1904.

> I am now able to inform you that the program of business to be submitted to the present Parliament will include in addition to the Budget and other ordinary requirements of that kind any necessary legislation upon the matters and lines embraced in the Ballarat platform of 1903 or since arising out of the action of the House.

> I may mention among the subjects that we hope to deal with some of them being already advanced more than one stage:

> 1.   White Australia

> 2.   Iron Bounty

---

[82] *Caucus Minutes*, 29 June 1905.

3.   Preferential Trade

4.   Rural development

5.   Navigation

6.   High Commissioner

7.   Tariff Commission Reports

8.   Trade Marks

9.   Fraudulent Marks

10.   Papua

11.   Quarantine

12.   Electoral requirements

13.   Population

14.   Old Age Pensions

15.   WA Survey

16.   Anti-Trust Bill

17.   Defence

18.   State Debts

We cannot hope to dispose of all those great problems but may be enabled to secure further consideration for these upon which legislative action is not yet desirable.[83]

---

[83] Papers of Alfred Deakin, National Library of Australia, Canberra. Watson to Deakin, 5 July 1905, MS 1540-16-392-s4-v

On 5 July 1905 Caucus voted to support Deakin and his legislative agenda stating:

> That this party having been informed through Mr Watson of the measures proposed to be submitted by Mr Deakin and agrees to give his ministry a general support during this parliament in the transaction of public business.[84]

Although no formal Alliance had been agreed to, some members regarded Watson's measure of support for Deakin as being potentially dangerous to the standing of the Party in the electorate. These members were jolted into action not only by the current arrangement, but also because of an implication contained in Watson's, previously quoted, letter to Deakin of 22 June 1905 where Watson wrote, "I feel that many moderate people who are a little afraid of us would rally to your support if given an opportunity. The Labor Party would become practically identical with the Protectionists."[85] Labor had again abandoned its platform, however there were Caucus members who tried to save the party some respectability by moving a motion, a copy of which was to be sent to Deakin, stating, "It must be clearly understood that the Labor Party acts as an independent party."[86] Incredibly, the motion was put to a vote and was lost. On 5 June 1905 Labor had for all intents and purposes become the labourist faction of Deakin's Protectionists. A footnote in the Caucus minutes recorded that, "... the members voting against the amendment being of the opinion that the independence of the Party was not in question."

Labor had in effect endorsed Deakin's policy agenda, abandoned their own platform as well as agreeing to grant immunity to sitting

---

[84] *Caucus Minutes*, 5 July 1905.
[85] <u>Papers of Alfred Deakin</u>, National Library of Australia, Canberra. Watson to Deakin, 22 June 1905, MS 1540-16-392-s4-v.
[86] *Caucus Minutes*, 5 July 1905.

Protectionist members at the following election. The integrity of the Party was shattered and those members who voted for the Alliance and against this motion also placed themselves in direct breach of Labor's Pledge. A majority of Caucus may have believed that the independence of the party was not in question, however the State organisations were united in their condemnation of Labor's participation in the Alliance.

The Third Commonwealth Political Labor Conference was held in July 1905 and immediately became enmeshed in the Alliance debate,[87] with the delegates from the parliamentary wing and the members of the wider labour movement being polarised in their views on the issue, with Conference moving quickly to negate any moves by the parliamentary wing to enter alliances with any other party. The first shot was fired by the Victorian PLC secretary Patrick Heagney who vigorously attacked the Alliance of the previous year and moved a motion to amend the federal pledge:

> After the words 'Caucus meeting' add the words 'and not to form any Alliance, coalition, or combination without such Alliance, coalition or combination having first obtained the sanction of the combined Labour organisations, to be determined by a special interstate conference.[88]

Heagney's motion was clear and unequivocal and reflected the concerns of the wider labour movement and in defence of his motion stated:

> ... an Alliance such as had taken place between the Labor Party and Mr Isaacs was subversive of the best interests of the movement. ... [and although] Mr Watson had carried

---

[87] The Third Commonwealth Political Labor Conference was held just after Caucus adopted their course of action.

[88] Australian Labor Party. <u>Third Commonwealth Political Labour Conference</u>. Melbourne, July 1905. p.19.

out his work with great skill under difficult circumstances, the Alliance was unwise when it attempted to obtain immunity from attack for those in the Alliance who were not Labor members.[89]

Supporting Heagney, Billson was of the view that, 'The great enemy to the cause was the man who was as good as a Labor man, and in the Alliance, there had been individuals of that stamp.'[90'] Billson's reasoning was also followed by Senator Turley from Queensland who was firmly of the view that, '... alliances, so far as he knew them, had done no good for the Labor Party. The men who came in with the Labor Party generally did so to get in out of the wet.'[91] Senator Turley, after speaking against the Alliance, then stated, '... the Alliance that Mr Watson had entered into had not affected the platform at all'.[92] Senator O'Keefe was also of the view that, '... the Alliance had not trenched on a plank of the party'.[93]

The Alliance proposals hit a raw nerve with the wider labour movement and highlighted the divide that existed between the parliamentary wing and the respective State organisations and the wider labour movement. Riley, a NSW delegate, stated, 'No Alliance should be countenanced which did not meet with the views of the various organisations.'[94]. Similarly, Lamond another NSW delegate declared, '... the Labor party ought not to join any Alliance or coalition without having first obtained the sanction of the State executives.'[95]

---

[89] ibid
[90] ibid., p.15.
[91] ibid., p.19.
[92] ibid.
[93] ibid., p.20.
[94] ibid.
[95] ibid.

Unsurprisingly, the parliamentary delegates did not share this view. Watson was adamant that the course he had taken and the decision to enter into an Alliance was not only justified but essential:

> The view I take is that the organisations outside lay down the policy upon which the Party is to work and decide what the platform should be. They arrange the Pledge for each candidate to take before he submits himself for election. But once the man is in parliament, they have to trust to his judgement to carry out their work. The Alliance at any rate prevented a fusion of the two other parties, who could thus have presented a solid phalanx to Labor.[96]

Watson's main reason for entering the Alliance was to 'prevent a fusion' of the two non-Labor parties. Watson's reasoning is somewhat disingenuous because during the early Alliance period Deakin and a large section of the radical Protectionists had no intention of 'fusing' with Reid. Spence agreed with his leader stating, '... organisations formed the policy, selected candidates, and did other work; but once their own men were in the House, they must trust them to carry out the platform.'[97]

Spence's assertion to 'trust them [parliamentary members] to carry out the platform' held about as much weight as Watson's 'Fusion argument', as Labor had done everything in its power, up to that point, to enter into alliances that negated its ability to actively pursue the platform.

At the conclusion of the Alliance debate, Heagney's original motion was amended and the conference passed a compromise resolution stating, 'That the Federal Labor Party should not enter into any Alliance that would extend beyond the then existing

---

[96] <u>ibid.</u>, p.19.
[97] <u>ibid.</u>, p.20

Parliament, nor grant nor promise immunity from opposition at election time.'[98]

Watson disagreed with Conference and wrote to Caucus:

> I may say primarily that the view I have held since the inception of Labor in politics is that the organisations should decide in conference what the policy of the movement should be and lay down such conditions as may be necessary to ensure the solidarity of the Party. Once the Party enters parliament it alone should, by its corporate voice, decide the course to be taken in any particular emergency. Having chosen its captains, the party outside should be prepared to trust to their guidance while the battle continues.[99]

In the remaining fifteen months of the second parliament the immunity issue continued to cause problems for Watson because he could not guarantee Deakin that Labor would not stand candidates in non-Labor members' electorates at future elections. In fact, Watson's immunity stance came back to haunt him at the general election of December 1906 when the Ballarat Labour League, holding true to their resolution to Watson of July 1905, that it was, 'their intention to oppose Deakin at the next election',[100] endorsed a young Jim Scullin to stand against him. Scullin was ultimately unsuccessful in his bid to unseat the Prime Minister, but the intention of the State organisation and rank and file members was clear, they did not want an Alliance that compromised their effectiveness to conduct elections or that negatively impacted on

---

[98] ibid., pp.19-20.

[99] Papers of John Christian Watson, National Library of Australia, Canberra. Watson to Caucus, MS 451, Series 1 correspondence, 1903-1941

[100] *Caucus Minutes*, July 27 1905.

the platform. In a private and confidential letter to Deakin after the election, Watson praised the Prime Minister but attacked his party for standing a man against him, "I need hardly say that I am glad you were returned, as I thought it was a great mistake to run a man against you at all."[101]

Watson may still have been upset about the Conference's decision about Labor entering alliances, however he should not have so openly criticised his party to his main rival. The Third Commonwealth Political Labor Conference played a pivotal role in ensuring federal Labor's survival as an independent political party, for it provided the members of the parliamentary wing with a veritable 'wakeup call' that jolted them back into reality. The Conference served to remind the political wing that they were members of a vibrant political movement with a strong support base, that had a legitimate claim to pursue government in its own right. The effect of the Conference was highlighted in Labor's move away from alliances, towards focusing on the platform and in the remaining six months of 1905 Labor picked up where it had left off before the removal from office of Watson's government in August 1904.

State Owned Steamers and the Nationalisation of Australia's Sugar Industry

In August 1905 Spence moved a motion for a state-owned steamer operation in line with plank 2 of the platform calling for the establishment of a select committee:

> ... to make full inquiry as to the advisability of the Federal Government owning and controlling a fleet of steamers, for the carriage of mails, passengers and cargo between

---

[101] Papers of Alfred Deakin, National Library of Australia, Canberra. Watson to Deakin, 17 December 1906, MS 1540-15-656-s1-v.

Australia and the United Kingdom.[102]

Spence's motion was subject to numerous amendments[103] but was approved by both Houses who subsequently turned the Committee into a Royal Commission, the majority report of which advocated the establishment of a Commonwealth owned and operated shipping line in line with plank 4 of Labor's platform. Labor's drive to enact plank 2 of the platform was further enhanced when on 18 September Senator Givens moved a motion for the nationalisation of Australia's sugar industry:

> That, in the opinion of the Senate, the refining and wholesale distribution of sugar within the Commonwealth being almost entirely controlled by one large corporation, constitutes a monopoly which is inimical to the best interests of those engaged in the production of raw sugars, and the citizens of the Commonwealth generally; and this Senate affirms the desirableness of nationalising the said monopoly, so as to secure to the people of the Commonwealth the whole of the benefits accruing therefrom.[104]

Labor's motion was subject to vigorous debate in the Senate about the pros and cons of Labor's socialist agenda and on 20 December 1905 the motion was resolved in the affirmative.[105] Labor's Senators carried the fight for the platform to the Government on many fronts also successfully moving for the establishment of a government owned cable service and life assurance office. Labor's success was tempered somewhat by the fact that very few initiatives

---

[102] *C.P.D.*, Vol. XXV, 10 August 1905, p.812.
[103] Deakin's amendment-ibid, p.814; Robinson's amendment - ibid, p.817; Thomas' amendment - *C.P.D.*, Vol. XXVI, 24 August 1905, p.1436

[104] *C.P.D.*, Vol. XXVII, 28 September 1905, p.2893.
[105] *C.P.D.*, Vol. XXX, 20 December 1905, p.7456.

reached the statute book, however even this being the case, Labor was once again advocating change in line with its stated platform and policies.

White Australia and the Nationalisation of Monopolies

In the House Labor also moved to strengthen its commitment and support for plank 1 of the platform relating to the 'Maintenance of a White Australia' with input during debate on the *Contract Immigrants Act* 1905, the Immigration Restriction Amendment Act 1905 and the *Pacific Islanders Labourers Act* 1906.

Labor's socialist leanings were the subject of increasing comment throughout Australia and attack by opponents in the Parliament, however the party was undeterred by political developments on this front and looked forward to defending their 'socialist' credentials at the federal election that would be held in December 1906. Labor's motions in the Senate to nationalise monopolies were consolidated on 16 August 1906 when the party moved to enact plank 4 of the platform by introducing legislation calling for a referendum on the question of nationalisation of monopolies when Senator Pearce moved:

> That leave be given to bring in a Bill for an Act to provide for an alteration of the Constitution for granting power to Parliament to make laws providing for the nationalisation of monopolies with respect to production, manufacture, trade and commerce.[106]

Labor had progressed to a point in the Parliament where it now actively sought to introduce legislation to enact the platform. Deakin was preparing for an election at the end of 1906 and the proposed Bill was an ideal vehicle to raise the profile of Labor's

---

[106] *C.P.D.*, Vol. XXXIII, 16 August 1906, p.2894.

commitment to its platform initiatives and to heighten awareness of its socialist character. The debate on the proposal primarily centred on the merits of socialism versus individualism and on what actually constituted a monopoly. Senator De Largie echoed Senator Pearce's comments and provided an outline as to why Labor viewed itself as a socialist party pursuing the nationalisation of monopolies:

> Whilst the rich are undoubtedly becoming richer the poor are becoming poorer. The chasm between the rich and the poor is becoming wider ... We therefore have to concentrate our attention on the question - how can we prevent the increase of such an evil in Australia? It is because the Labor Party think that this concentration of capital in the hands of individuals at the expense of society as a whole can only be lessened by the means of wealth production being in the hands of the public instead of being privately owned that we favour this policy ... It is not a question of men. It is far deeper than personalities. It is a question of great principles; and believing as I do that if an opportunity were given to the people of this country to express their opinion by referendum, they would give us the power under the Constitution to take over monopolies, which would be better in the hands of the Government than in private control.[107]

Senator De Largie's hope that the people of Australia would be provided with an opportunity to vote at a referendum on the matter was dashed when the Senate, in a tied vote of thirteen votes for and thirteen against resolved the motion in the negative.[108] The Bill was dropped from the legislative agenda and although unsuccessful in passing the initiative, the party turned its attention

---

[107] *C.P.D.*, Vol. XXXV, 4 October 1906, p.6041.
[108] ibid., p.6060.

to the federal election that had been announced by Deakin for 12 December 1906.

4 THE END OF ALLIANCES

On 12 December 1906 Australians went to the polls and the result in the House saw the Deakin Protectionists win seventeen seats, the Anti-Socialists thirty-two seats and Labor twenty-six seats,[109] a net gain of two seats. In the Senate Labor won five seats taking their numbers to fifteen, the Anti-Socialists twelve seats taking their numbers to seventeen and Deakin's Protectionists were again hit hard only winning one seat, with only four Senators. Deakins early election prognosis proved prophetic, as his 'party of the centre' was squeezed by both Labor and Reid. However, Deakin's losses were Labor's gains and Labor found itself in a position of strength with sufficient numbers in the House to lead a coalition government with Deakin's support.

Watson was in an excellent position to pursue a mandate as Deakin would not join Reid, this was despite the fact that Reid's Anti-Socialists were the largest single party in the House. This development also provided further weight to discount Watson's earlier rationale for entering into an Alliance 'to stop the fusion of the non-Labor parties'. The result was positive for Labor and Watson was now in a position to discuss with Caucus the formation of a Labor government. However, what may have seemed apparent to Labor members and ordinary rank and file supporters

[109] Of the Anti-socialists, nine could be described as the Tariff Reformers of the Opposition 'corner'. Five of the latter could also be counted on to give Deakin a fair measure of support, so that in contemporary accounts he is sometimes credited with twenty-two followers; in Sawer, 1956, op cit., p.62

was negated by Watson, who on 17 December, only five days after the election, and without holding discussions with Caucus wrote to Deakin urging him to stay on as Prime Minister:

> ... you must, I think, see the tariff through at least. A number of so called Anti- Socialists are pledged to a protectionist tariff, and there is no combination could be got together outside the present Ministry which could do that work as well. I don't think it is necessary to look further ahead than that at present. As you know, our party is not anxious for office unless a program worth having could be carried through and I'm not too sure that in the Parliament as at present constituted there is much chance of carrying much of the Labor party's program. If not, we must be patient. At least you can rely that we shall do nothing against your Ministry while engaged in altering the tariff and in carrying other matters of a Democratic nature.[110]

Watson's letter is amazing considering he did not discuss his position with the members of Caucus or the party in general and as Faulkner and MacIntyre observed, 'Watson was jumping the gun here - Caucus had not at that stage discussed the implications of the election outcome at all.'[111] Watson's statement in his letter to Deakin, 'As you know, our party is not anxious for office unless a program worth having could be carried through', is incredible in the context of the times. Labor had held office for only a short period in 1904, the parliamentary and the administrative wings of the Party had been at each other's throats over the previous couple of years with respect of alliances and kowtowing to Deakin, and Watson's bold assertion that Labor did not want to govern because it would not be able to implement a program 'worth having' was a

---

[110] <u>Papers of Alfred Deakin</u>, National Library of Australia, Canberra, Canberra. Watson to Deakin, 17 December 1906, ms 1540-15-656-sl-v.
[111] Faulkner, <u>op cit</u>., p.35.

gross dereliction of his duty as leader of the party. The Articles of Alliance of an earlier time and the content of legislation that had been passed since 1901 had shown that Labor's legislative policy agenda with respect of implementing the platform had always taken a back seat to the interests of Deakin, who Watson supported. Strong leadership was required; however, Watson had shown that he was not the person to lead the party to government. Watson simply was not up to the challenge of leading Labor into power to enact the platform. On 20 December Deakin replied to Watson's letter:

> ... the coming parliament is going to repeat the history of the last parliament step by step ... This means that Reid or you will be sent for very soon. Whether you like it or not your party will then have either to take office or go into opposition.[112]

Deakin also discussed the fiscal issue and stated that, 'Protection is safe in any case and probably more easily secured if we were out of office.'[113]   Deakin's response is unequivocal, he believed that Watson or Reid would become the next Prime Minister. Watson had a duty to discuss these developments with his Caucus colleagues, however he chose not to and on 27 December he responded to Deakin urging him to stay on and resolve the tariff issue:

> Now as to the future: I think you're altogether wrong as to Protection being 'safe in any case'. If Reid or any other leader on that side assumes office, the Ministry must include a number of Free Traders, which means that only 'anomalies' will be dealt with, and that Protection in a large

---

[112] <u>Papers of Alfred Deakin</u>, National Library of Australia, Canberra. Deakin to Watson, 20 December 1906, MS 1540-15-665-v.

[113] <u>ibid</u>.

sense will be lost sight of or ignored. If a coalition took place immediately with our Party something of the same sort must happen, though in a lesser degree. Therefore, it seems imperative from a Protectionist standpoint that you should retain office, at least until the tariff is dealt with.[114]

La Nauze has contended that Watson did not want to split the party on the fiscal issue commenting, 'There was honest shrewdness in these [Watson's] evasive tactics. As a Protectionist, Watson knew well that he had a problem with his own party ... as a Party leader, he saw nothing to be gained by Labor's holding office in the minority; it led to nothing but compromise.'[115] La Nauze was correct about Watson being a protectionist, however the remainder of his thesis holds little credibility. The election results placed Watson, as the leader of the party, in a position to negotiate with Deakin for Labor to assume government. Coalition governments had become a feature of the Federal Parliament up to this point and contrary to La Nauze's assertion, there was plenty to be gained by Labor assuming office, pursuing the platform and espousing Labor policy being the major drivers behind forming a government, even in a coalition capacity.

Labor had not been established to pick and choose when it would be convenient for it to govern, when the opportunity presented itself, it had an obligation to do it. Watson was in a position to deal with Deakin, firstly, to pass the Protectionist legislation on the fiscal issue and secondly, in response to Labor passing the tariff Bill, that Deakin support Labor's mandate to govern, as well as providing

---

[114] <u>Papers of John Christian Watson</u>, National Library of Australia, Canberra. J.C Watson to Deakin, 27 December 1906, MS 451, Series 1 correspondence, 1903-1941. 158 La Nauze, <u>op cit.</u>, p.421.

[115] <u>Papers of Alfred Deakin</u>, National Library of Australia, Canberra. Deakin to Watson, 20 December 1906, MS 1540-15-665-v.

support in the House and in the Senate for enacting elements of Labor's platform. Watson, however negated any possibility of Labor taking the lead stating, "As to our taking office, without a coalition it is out of the question, and what prospect is there of getting a coalition that will enable us to realise any important portion of our program."[116]

The nuances of completing such a deal with Deakin may have been difficult, however at no stage in discussions between the two men did Watson indicate that he wanted to lead the country or place Labor in a position where its policy platform could have a maximum impact. As the leader of the party Watson had a duty to enact the platform and inform his colleagues of his intentions: he failed on both counts. On 19 February 1907, nearly two months after the election, Caucus finally met to discuss the election, it had not previously had an opportunity to discuss the impact of the election and its implications for a Labor Government. The minutes of the meeting show that, '... a discussion took place on the present political position, but no decision was arrived at.'[117]

As Labor leader, Watson should have called a special meeting of Caucus as soon as practicable after the election, as had occurred in April 1904 when Deakin resigned, to discuss all the options open to the party before speaking with Deakin. However, as has already been noted, Watson chose to ignore Caucus and instead chose Labor's course of action himself, ensuring Deakin remained Prime Minister and markedly reduced Labor's opportunity to legislate for its platform.

The Parliament resumed in February 1907 with Deakin leading a minority Government with Labor support: Labor's twenty-six were

---

[116] <u>Papers of Alfred Deakin</u>, National Library of Australia, Canberra. Watson to Deakin, 27 December 1906, MS 1540-15-671-s2-v.

[117] *Caucus Minutes*, February 19, 1907.

supporting Deakin's seventeen. Watson remained as leader until October when he resigned and announced that he would retire from the Parliament at the next election, citing ill health and stress as the major reasons for his decision. Watson's health was a key factor in his decision, however there was also a 'growing dissatisfaction within Caucus about Labor's tactical approach under Watson'[118] with Faulkner stating, 'Frazer and Ted Findley, a Victorian senator, were conspicuous among a Caucus ginger group (the first FPLP faction?) who wanted Watson to be more assertive there were not enough concessions, they felt in return for the consistent Caucus support.'[119]

Another reason for Watson's resignation, directly linked to a growing dissatisfaction within Caucus, was also posited by Sawer, 'There is some reason for thinking that health was not the only ground for his resignation. The course of events shows that the Labor Party was becoming increasingly aggressive and ambitious in its tactics and aims, and impatient of the arrangement with Deakin, which Watson had managed with great tact; the temperament Watson displayed in debates suggests that he might have preferred to have kept Deakin in Office.'[120] In truth Watson's resignation was probably a culmination of all of these factors. The only certainty was that Labor would have a new leader after Watson's resignation. There were four nominations for the leadership, Mr A. Fisher[121]; Mr W. M. Hughes[122]; Mr E.L. Batchelor[123] and Mr W.G. Spence[124]. Batchelor declined the nomination and withdrew his nomination whilst Spence, who

---

[118] Faulkner, op cit., p.37.

[119] Ibid.

[120] Sawer, 1956, op cit., p.64.

[121] Fisher was nominated by Dr Maloney, seconded O'Malley. *Caucus Minutes*, October 30, 1907.

[122] Hughes was nominated by D. Hall, seconded T. Brown. ibid.

[123] Batchelor was nominated by G. McGregor, seconded W. Storey. ibid.

[124] Spence was nominated by P. Lynch, seconded D. Watkins. ibid.

'never seemed quite at home'[125] in politics had few supporters within the party especially so as he was against Fisher and Hughes who both had solid support. Whilst Caucus deliberated, Fisher and Hughes 'had a game of billiards',[126] and after an exhaustive ballot Fisher was elected as the new leader.[127] The major factor in Fisher's victory was that Hughes was more closely linked to Watson and 'Caucus members discontented with Watson's attitude to the Deakin government voted for Fisher.'[128] If elements within the parliamentary party and the wider Labour movement expected Fisher to immediately confront Deakin about forming a Labor coalition government; they would be disappointed as Labor continued to support Deakin through to the summer recess of 1907.

Parliament resumed in March 1908, however Labor attitudes had changed over the summer break and within a month of the Parliament resuming, the Deakin Government found itself in trouble. On 9 April 1908 Deakin attempted to introduce government business, however Labor's Webster challenged his motion and moved an amendment calling for a Royal Commission into the operation of the Post Office, 'That all the words after 'That' be left out, with a view to insert in lieu thereof the words, 'a Royal Commission be appointed to inquire into and report upon the Postal, Telegraph, and Telephone systems of the Commonwealth, and the working thereof.'[129]

Labor had been dissatisfied with workers' wages and conditions in the Postmaster General's Department and wanted the matter

---

[125] Fitzhardinge, op cit., p. 120.

[126] McMullin, 1991, op cit., p.63.

[127] No details of voting figures were published in the press, which did not even note that the leadership had been contested. see Caucus Minutes, October 30, 1907.

[128] McMullin, 1991, op cit. p.63.

[129] *C.P.D.*, Vol. XLV, 9 April 1908, p.10,406.

reviewed. The motion also provided an opportunity for anti-Deakin elements within Labor, led by Frazer, to force the issue of Labor's claims on government. Deakin had made it clear to Watson after the 1906 election that his government would not accept 'even a check without taking it as a challenge'[130], and Webster's motion had been the first 'check' to his government since that time. Deakin sought the reversal of Webster's motion, as he believed that the motion was ostensibly a vote of no confidence in his government. After the vote on Webster's motion was taken, Fisher and Watson began discussions with Deakin, and Watson was given responsibility by Fisher to negotiate with Deakin over the fate of Deakin's government. On the 10th April Caucus held a special meeting to discuss developments about a Coalition.[131] Caucus endorsed Watson's coalition proposal[132] as well as passing a resolution to adjourn Webster's original motion for a royal commission, '... provided the Government proceeded solely with the Tariff until it passed into law.'[133] Deakin's Government remained but Labor had again placed itself in conflict with the State organisations by advocating another Alliance.

<u>Old-Age Pensions</u>

Fisher continued to support Deakin, however on 19 March 1908 he successfully moved a motion drawing the attention of the Government to the urgent need of a Commonwealth system of Old Age Pensions in line with plank 3 of the platform.[134] Fisher's

---

[130] <u>Papers of Alfred Deakin</u>, National Library of Australia, Canberra. Deakin to Watson, 20 December 1906, MS 1540-15-665-v.

[131] *Caucus Minutes*, 14 April 1908.

[132] The vote was carried by twenty votes to thirteen and the meeting was adjourned to the following day where Watson and Fisher held talks with Deakin and 'conveyed to him the decision of the Party. ALP, *Caucus Minutes*, 14 April 1908.

[133] <u>ibid</u>.

[134] See; *C.P.D.*, Vol. XLIV, 19 March 1908, pp.9301-9351.

motion was followed some six weeks later by the introduction of the Invalid and Old Age Pensions Bill by Deakin that would enact plank 3 of the platform that called for the introduction of 'Old Age Pensions'. On 3 June 1908 Fisher outlined his pleasure at the introduction of the legislation, 'It is a pleasure to myself and the members of my party - and, indeed, to the whole of the members of the Parliament - that we are able to deal with this question at the present time ... It is a matter for congratulation that the mother of Parliaments has seen fit, in respect to old age pensions, to copy the example of her progeny in Australia, and that, although, this is still not all that I or the party with which I am associated would like it to be, it is an advance upon any legislation of the kind passed in any other part of the world.'[135]

Fisher was successful in ensuring the passage of a core plank in Labor's platform, a plank that was plank 4 in Labor's original platform of 1901. The passage of the *Invalid and Old Age Pensions Act 1908* was the first real example of 'support in return for concessions' in enacting a plank of the platform that Labor had achieved since 1901. Plank 4 of the platform, providing for Invalid and Old Age Pensions, was the only plank that Labor had successfully pursued that was not a part of any other party's policy manifesto of the time. The term 'support in return for concessions' is a descriptor that historians like McMullin have placed on Labor during this period.[136] However, as can be seen, this is misleading because although Labor members pursued the platform on a number of occasions, especially in the Senate, and provided input on legislation related to the platform, the only notable legislative success was the *Invalid and Old Age Pensions Act* 1908. There was certainly Labor support, but there were very few concessions, as Deakin did very little to advance Labor platform planks such as the

---

[135] *C.P.D.*, Vol. XLVI, 3 June 1908, pp.11933-4.
[136] See McMullin, 1991, <u>op cit</u>., pp. 15-49.

nationalisation initiatives whilst governing in a minority capacity.

Four days after the *Invalid and Old Age Pensions Act* 1908 came into effect the High Court delivered a judgement in the case of *King v Barger*[137] that had a dramatic impact on the validity of the 'New Protection' regime that was supported by all parties in the parliament.[138] New Protection was an important issue to Labor because the crux of the protection sought to ensure that workers were provided with fair and reasonable working conditions at their place of employment: the High Court's judgement effectively negated this right.[139] The High Court's decision placed pressure on Deakin to safeguard New Protection and he assured the House that the Government was committed to the policy of New Protection and that it, 'was only a question of the particular way they should proceed'[140] that was an issue.

The End of Alliances and the Emergence of the first Fisher Government

A month after the High Court's decision the Fourth Commonwealth Political Labour Conference was held in Brisbane and Conference successfully moved to install 'The New Protection' policy as plank 2 in the platform, however the major issue once again focussed on Labor's persistent flirtation with alliances. The Conference wasted little time to ensure that Labor would enter no future alliances or grant immunity to non-labor candidates at elections, passing the following resolution, 'That in the opinion of Conference the Party should not enter into any Alliance, nor grant, nor promise to any person immunity from opposition at any time.'[141]

---

[137] *King v Barger* 6 CLR 41.

[138] See Sawer, <u>op cit.</u>, p.83; La Nauze, <u>op cit.</u>, pp.435-8.

[139] The High Court verdict was a split 3-2 decision with Griffith, Barton and O'Connor voting to negate the effect of the New Protection regime.

[140] see; *C.P.D.*, Vol. XLV, 3 April 1908, p.10,132; and *C.P.D.*, Vol. XLVI, 26 May 1908, p.11,421.

Senator Findlay was one of the main advocates and a mover for the 'No Alliance' motion:

> We have been fighting against the 'good-as-Labor' men, and any Alliance formed invariably helps that tattered brigade of shreds and patches to a new lease of life, which is spent in insidiously trying to undermine Labour organisation ... Labor is an uncompromising Party which came into being because the workers were dissatisfied with Liberals. Should they then compromise with those people whose very inactivity and insincerity led to the birth of the Labor Party? The attitude I and my Victorian colleagues take up is that giving the power to the FPLP to form alliances and grant immunity - thereby tying the hands of the people outside - is acting contrary to the principles of democracy.[142]

The motion was overwhelmingly carried by delegates, by over two to one, and scuttled Fisher and Watson's plan for any Alliance. Watson was philosophical about the outcome and conceded that, '... the feeling of conference was against alliances, and that must be respected.'[143] Watson's conciliatory tone is perplexing in that both himself and Fisher must have been aware that Conference would most certainly move to halt the Alliance but they continued with Deakin regardless. An analysis of the time line from April to July 1908 shows that although Fisher and Watson may have been sincere, at least to Deakin, about an Alliance, their main concern was ensuring the tariff legislation was passed, new protection safeguarded and that old age pensions were placed on the agenda. The Alliance proposal merely being an inducement for Deakin to

---

[141] Findley, E., <u>Fourth Commonwealth Political Labour Conference</u>, Brisbane, July 6-10, 1908, p. 26.
[142] <u>ibid</u>.
[143] <u>ibid</u>. p.27.

continue. This scenario gains weight when one looks at the fact that during the period when the Alliance was to take place, there was no real movement by Labor to bring it into effect. In fact, Fisher wrote to Deakin at the end of the session in June 1908 urging him to stay on, 'I shall not be a party to your humiliation while you and I understand each other as at present ... I shall go further and say that no carping criticism shall be heard from me even though I may think you have taken a wrong course.'[144]

Parliament reassembled in September 1908 and Deakin introduced measures reviving the new protection regime by proposing an amendment to authorise legislation concerning, '... the employment and remuneration of Labour in any industry which in the opinion of the interstate Commission is protected by duties of Customs.'[145] There was no Interstate Commission in existence at this time, however it was proposed that it be established by legislation. Deakin's proposals were not greeted with enthusiasm by members of the party as it ran contrary to Labor's platform, and Labor's representatives on the New Protection Committee reported to Caucus on 4 November 1908 stating that in their opinion, '... the government memorandum on New Protection is unsatisfactory.'[146]

The negative response to Deakin's proposal provided the catalyst for Frazer to move a motion attacking Deakin's proposal and calling for Labor to withdraw support from the Government, 'That in the view of the attitude of the Government in relation to New Protection, Old Age Pensions, Immigration Restriction Act, Finance and other matters, the relations existing between the Party

---

[144] Papers of Alfred Deakin, National Library of Australia, Canberra. Watson to Deakin, 24 June 1908, MS 1540-15-824-v.
[145] New Protection - Memorandum relating to the proposed Amendment of the Constitution, Commonwealth Parliamentary Papers, 1908, Vol ii.
[146] *Caucus Minutes*, 4 November 1908.

and the Government should not continue.'[147]   Caucus passed Frazer's motion[148] and also moved that Fisher inform Deakin as soon as possible of the general terms of the decision of the party. No formal steps were taken to remove Deakin until 10 November when a vote amounting to one of no confidence in Deakin's government was carried in the House. On 10 November 1908 Caucus met in the morning and discussed strategy with Fisher reporting that, '... in the event of the Prime Minister moving a resolution, that the Executive were unanimously of the opinion that he should move the omission of all words after 'That".[149]

In the House Deakin moved a motion and Fisher moved the amendment so that the only word remaining of Deakin's original motion was the word 'That'. In the subsequent division on the motion Deakin's administration effectively came to an end with a vote of no confidence of forty-nine to thirteen. Deakin subsequently ended proceedings by replying, 'In order that the house may give full and profound attention to all the possible meanings that are to be found in the one word of my motion remaining, I propose to move that the House at its rising adjourn until Friday'.[150]

On 11 November Deakin and his ministers resigned and Deakin advised the Governor General to send for Fisher. On 13 November the first Fisher administration took office with Caucus electing members for ministerial duties and the Prime Minister (Fisher) allocating portfolios.[151]   A day before the Christmas recess

---

[147] ibid.

[148] ibid., The motion was passed with a majority of nineteen votes to seven with six pairs on each side.

[149] *Caucus Minutes*, 10 November 1908.

[150] *C.P.D.*, Vol. XLVIII, 10 November 1908, p.2140.

[151] On 12 November Caucus moved that 'we give effect to the resolution carried at the interstate conference at Melbourne 'That future Labor Ministers be recommended by the parliamentary party in Caucus' and that the 'party have

Labor introduced the Immigration Restriction Bill to further strengthen plank 1 of the platform that called for the 'Maintenance of White Australia'. The Bill sought to address the problem of ships smuggling Asiatics, especially Chinese, into Australia. On 10 December 1908, Batchelor outlined the main reason for the introduction of the Bill:

> I should like to remind honourable members that the principal Act has been in operation for seven years, and that during that time the education test for which it provides has been rigorously applied to all Asiatics, and particularly to Chinese, seeking to enter the Commonwealth ... the Chinese are exceedingly clever in evading or attempting to evade, the provisions of the Act, and are perhaps more anxious than are other Asiatics to enter Australia. In the natural course of events, the number of Asiatics now in the Commonwealth ought to be less than it was when the principal Act first came into force.[152]

The Bill was adjourned, and the Fisher Government entered into the Christmas recess on 11 December in a position they had not been in since 1904. The Parliament resumed a little over five months later and on 26 May 1909 the fourth session of the third parliament commenced. Unbeknown to Labor, Deakin had been rallying support of Opposition members to join a new Fusion Party to bring down the Labor Government. Deakin wrote to Fisher informing him of his new party's intentions, 'At a meeting of my party yesterday. I was authorised to intimate to you that support could no longer be confirmed.'[153]

---

every confidence in its leader, leaves the selection of his colleagues in his hands'.
[152] *C.P.D.*, Vol. XLVIII, 10 December 1908, p.3087.
[153] <u>Papers of Alfred Deakin</u>, National Library of Australia, Canberra. Deakin to Watson, undated correspondence 1909, MS 1540-16-595-s1-v.

On 27 May a formal motion amounting to one of no confidence was carried against the Fisher Government by thirty-nine votes to thirty.[154] Deakin had successfully fused all non-Labor parties to his cause and Labor once again found themselves in opposition. The Parliament erupted at Deakin's news, especially the Labor members, Hughes in particular was particularly scathing in his attack on Deakin:

> What a career his has been! In his hands, at various times, have rested the banners of every party in the country. He has proclaimed them all, he has held them all, he has betrayed them all.[155]

Last night the honourable member abandoned the finer resources of political assassination and resorted the bludgeon of the cannibal ... It was then that I heard from this side of the House some mention of Judas. I do not agree with that; it is not fair - to Judas, for whom there is this to be said, that he did not gag the man whom he betrayed, nor did he fail to hang himself afterwards.[156]

The second federal Labor Government had come to an abrupt, but not too unexpected end, via the endless wheeling and dealing of Deakin, and like Watson's first ministry Labor was not in power long enough to pass any legislation in relation to the platform and according to Fitzhardinge, 'Fisher's first government, even more than Watson's, was a mere interlude.'[157]

The remainder of the third Parliament took place in an atmosphere of mistrust and bitterness between Labor and Deakin, however Labor members approved the passage of amending legislation to strengthen plank 10 of the general platform related to

---

[154] *C.P.D.*, Vol. XLIX, 27 May 1909, p.126.
[155] ibid., p.114.
[156] *C.P.D.*, Vol. XLIX., 28 May 1909, pp.174-5.
[157] Fitzhardinge, op cit., p.175.

the provision of 'Old Age and Invalid Pensions' with the passage of the *Invalid and Old Age Pensions Act (No.1)* 1909, the *Invalid and Old Age Pensions Act (No.2)* 1909 and the *Old Age Pensions Appropriation Act* 1909. The most important measure introduced by Labor during this period was the Constitution Alteration Bill (Nationalisation of Monopolies) in line with plank 3 of the fighting and general platform. Labor had continually advocated the nationalisation of monopolies throughout the third Parliament, and despite the fact that they did not have the numbers to ensure its passage, they continued to press their claim on enacting plank 3 of the platform into law by calling for a national referendum on the issue. On 29 July 1909 Senator Pearce outlined the rationale for the Bill to the Senate:

> Some legal opinions of a very formidable character have been given, to the effect that the Commonwealth cannot nationalise trusts under the Constitution as it stands, unless the nationalisation of a particular monopoly is necessarily incidental to the carrying out of some powers under the Constitution. I quite recognise that those monopolies, which I, at any rate, desire that Parliament should have power to nationalise, are not incidental to carrying out any of the special powers of the Federal Constitution. It is, for that reason, necessary that we should seek to obtain power to enable us to nationalise monopolies.[158]

The Constitution Alteration Bill (Nationalisation of Monopolies) did not reach a division and the Bill lapsed at prorogation, and although unsuccessful in even reaching a division before the end of the Parliament, Labor was still fighting to implement key planks in its platform. The Bill was the last Labor foray into enacting a plank of the platform before Deakin prorogued the Parliament and

---

[158] *C.P.D.*, Vol. L, 29 July 1909, p.1759.

called a general election for 13 April 1910.

5 CONCLUSION

In the first Parliament, Labor's 'corner party' status was certainly warranted, however although never in the ascendancy its members acted with conviction in pursuing Labor's stated platform goals. This conviction was nowhere better demonstrated than in relation to the enactment and maintenance of plank 1 of the platform calling for a 'White Australia'. Labor members passionately advocated for legislation such as the *Immigration Restriction Act* 1901 and the *Pacific Islanders Labourers Act* 1901. The support of legislation supporting plank 1 was soon followed by support for the *Commonwealth Franchise Act* 1902 that provided for 'adult suffrage' and enacted plank 2 of the platform.

In 1903 Labor members supported the passage of the *Patents Act* 1903 to enact plank 9 of the platform. In the area of Defence, the *Defence Act* 1903 was passed with Labor support, albeit with major differences over the issue of conscription. The passage of the *Defence Act* 1903 laid the foundation for the establishment of a citizen volunteer force in line with plank 5 of Labor's platform. Labor's support for legislation did not automatically make it a rubber stamp for all of the Government's proposals. Deakin's *Naval Defence Act* 1903 came under sustained pressure from Labor members who called for the establishment of an Australian owned and controlled Navy in line with plank 5 of the platform and the call for Australia to cut the links with the mother country. Labor's attempts to amend the *Naval Act* 1903 were not successful, however what was of significance during this period was Labor's wholesale pursuit of plank 2 of the platform during the debate on the Conciliation and Arbitration Bill 1903. Labor advocated strongly for industrial relations reform in line with the industrial arbitration planks in the platform to the extent that Deakin dropped the legislation from the legislative agenda.

The first Parliament provided Labor with a valuable insight into what was required to pursue the platform. Labor was a bit player in the House wedged between Deakin's Protectionists and Reid's Free Traders, however Labor members were undaunted by the fact that they were only a small party in the Parliament, and on issues related to the platform they pursued them with vigour and were successful in ensuring the passage of planks relating to 'White Australia', 'adult suffrage', 'patent' and a 'citizen defence force'. Labor had come of age and had proven to the wider labour movement that it could hold its own at a national level.

Labor's position and its influence in the Parliament was strengthened after the 1903 election when it won twenty-five seats in the House and fourteen in the Senate. Labor were no longer a 'comer party', they were a party that were numerically on a level par with Deakin's Protectionists and Reid's Free Traders. Labor's influence in the Parliament was reflected in the Senate where it successfully passed two motions to enact plank 4 of the platform calling for the 'Nationalisation of Monopolies'. Labor introduced a motion calling for the nationalisation of Tobacco, the primary purpose of which was to fund 'Old Age Pensions' in line with plank 3 of the platform. Labor's success in passing the motion was then followed with another motion calling for the establishment of a Federal Iron works in line with plank 4 of the platform. The success of the motions sent a clear signal that Labor would actively pursue the platform now that its numbers and influence had increased in the Parliament.

Labor began strongly and in April 1904 Watson became the World's first Labor Prime Minister when Deakin resigned his commission over a Labor amendment to the Conciliation and Arbitration Bill that sought to include state government employees within the federal system. Labor's rise to power was remarkable, however it did not enjoy the support of either Deakin or Reid and governed in a minority capacity. The advent of a minority Labor Government also brought with it a strong push from within the parliamentary wing of the party to form an Alliance with Deakin. The Alliance proposals certainly reflected the state of play in the Parliament at the time, however there were also proposals to grant immunity to non-Labor members at elections, and instead of pursuing the platform whilst in Government, Labor became entangled in debate surrounding alliances. In the Parliament Labor continued with the Conciliation and Arbitration Bill and they were eventually removed from office in August after a deft piece of parliamentary manoeuvring by Deakin during debate over the Conciliation and Arbitration Bill. Labor's grasp on power was tenuous but it had shown that it could occupy the Treasury benches and govern in its own right.

The fall of the Watson Government also lead to the parliamentary wing of the party attempting to enter alliances with Deakin to ostensibly make the party the labourist faction of Deakin's Protectionists. Labor grappled with the issue of alliances for the next twelve months until delegates at the Third Commonwealth Political Labour Conference in July 1905 voted to officially put an end to Labor's flirtation with alliances. The Alliance period saw Labor abandon the platform, however after the Third Commonwealth Political Labour Conference the parliamentary wing were brought back to earth, and immediately began setting their sights on pursuing the platform. In August, Labor moved a motion in line with plank 2 of the platform calling for Federal Government to prepare a report on the feasibility of establishing a

State-owned steamer operation. The motion was passed by both Houses and the subsequent inquiry was turned into a Royal Commission, whose majority report advocated the establishment of a Commonwealth owned and operated shipping line.

In September, Labor successfully passed a motion in the Senate calling for the nationalisation of the sugar industry in line with plank 2 of the platform. Labor Senators continued pursuing the platform on many fronts and also successfully introduced a motion calling for the establishment of a government owned cable service and life assurance office. In August 1906 Labor introduced legislation in the senate calling for a referendum on the issue of 'Nationalisation of Monopolies' in line with plank 2 of the platform. The issue of socialism had been at the forefront of political debate and Labor moved to consolidate its position and in a heated debate on the subject the Senate produced a tied vote of thirteen votes for and thirteen votes against, with the proposal being resolved in the negative.

Labor Senators were clearly the more active of the two chambers in pursuit of the platform, however in the House Labor did move to strengthen its commitment to plank 1 of the platform supporting the *Contract Immigrants Act* 1905, the *Immigration Restriction Amendment Act* 1905 and the *Pacific Islanders Labourers Act* 1906. Labor's development during the second Parliament was critically important to the evolution of the party during the period. It had entered the Parliament with an increased majority in both chambers and its numerical advance was reflected in its pursuit of the platform, especially in the Senate where it used its numbers to pursue key planks in the platform and although nearly imploding over the issue of alliances with Deakin, it worked its way through difficult issues to where it again was placing pressure on the Government and moving to introduce legislation to enact the platform whilst supporting Government measures that strengthened planks of the platform.

In December 1906 Labor were again at the polls and they increased their numbers in the House to twenty-six and in the Senate to fifteen. Watson, as leader of the party was now in a strong position to negotiate with Deakin for support for a Labor Government, however in what became an absurd situation, Watson, without consulting Caucus, agreed that Labor's twenty-six would support Deakin's seventeen.

In October 1907 Watson resigned as leader and was replaced by Fisher. In April 1908 Labor was able to bring down Deakin' s Government, however Fisher and Watson chose to enter an Alliance with Deakin and keep him in power with a condition of the Alliance that Deakin legislate for plank 3 of the platform and introduce Old Age and Invalid pensions. In June Deakin introduced the Invalid and Old Age Pensions Bill into the Parliament and it was passed with Labor's full support.

In July, Labor's Fourth Commonwealth Political Conference again condemned Labor's pursuit of alliances. Fisher continued to support Deakin until November when he withdrew Labor's support for the Government and on 13 November 1908 Fisher became Labor's second Prime Minister. Labor wasted little time in introducing the Immigration Restriction Bill into the Parliament to strengthen plank 1 of the platform before the Christmas recess. Unfortunately for Labor, it was never able to enact the Bill, for Deakin had been busy during the recess and had forged an Alliance with the opposition members into a new Fusion Party and he brought down the Government when Parliament resumed in May 1909.

In terms of legislative achievement, the record of Labor enacting planks in the platform was quite notable given the circumstances in which the party operated. The key platform achievements were the support for White Australia, Adult Suffrage, Patents, Defence and the support for the introduction of Old Age Pensions. In fact, Old Age Pensions was the only plank that Labor was committed to passing that the other parties did not already have on their respective legislative agendas in the first instance. Labor's ability to influence legislation in line with the platform changed when Labor strengthened its position in the Senate after successive elections, where it used its numbers and growing influence in that chamber to successfully pass motions to pursue stated planks of the platform, especially in relation to the nationalisation of monopolies. Thus, in its first decade Labor's pursuit of the platform was a mixed one. Labor's early enthusiasm in supporting key platform planks; reluctance associated with Watson's temerity; strong Senate efforts and ultimate revival under Fisher!

The first ten years provided an enormous challenge for all those involved at all levels of the party and although emerging somewhat battered and bruised at the end of the decade, Labor had learnt valuable lessons that would hold it in positive stead for what lay ahead. The real test for Labor in the pursuit of the platform would come if they were ever elected to govern the country in their own right and in the first decade of federation no party could lay claim to this honour. The year of 1910 would prove to be pivotal in the history of the party and the wider labour movement.

6 APPENDICES

Appendix 1 -Australian Labor Party Federal Platform 1901

1. That the Party be named 'The Commonwealth Labor Party'.
2. That the Party sit in each house on the cross benches.
3. That the executive of the Party be elected annually and that it consists of a Chairman, a Vice Chairman, a Secretary, an Assistant Secretary, and three members. The secretary and Assistant Secretary to act as Whips in their respective Houses.
4. That members of the Federal Parliament not elected on the Labor ticket be admitted on two thirds vote of the party and on signing the Federal Labor platform.
5. That current politics take precedence at all Caucus meetings of the party.
6. That the Commonwealth Parliamentary or fighting Labor Platform consist of the following planks, viz:
    a. A White Australia
    b. Adult Suffrage
    c. Old Age pensions
    d. A citizen army
    e. Compulsory arbitration

The committee consider that as some of the members from the smaller States are opposed to the National Referendum, and as the question is not likely to come up in an acute form for some time, it would be unwise to insist upon its inclusion in our platform at present. Members, however, who have pledged themselves to that plank should be quite free to advocate it.[159]

---

[159] *Caucus Minutes*, 20 May 1901.

Appendix 2 - Australian Labor Party Federal Platform 1902

Fighting Platform

1. Maintenance of a White Australia.
2. Compulsory Arbitration.
3. Old Age Pensions.
4. Nationalisation of Monopolies.
5. Citizen Defence Force
6. Restriction of Public Borrowing.
7. Navigation Laws.

General Platform

1. Maintenance of a White Australia.
2. Compulsory Arbitration to settle industrial disputes, with provision for the exclusion of the legal profession.
3. Old Age Pensions.
4. Nationalisation of Monopolies.
5. Citizen Military Force and Australian owned Navy.
6. Restriction of Public Borrowing.
7. Navigation Laws to provide
   a) for the protection of Australian shipping against unfair competition
   b) registration of all vessels engaged in the coastal trade
   c) the efficient manning of vessels
   d) the proper supply of life-saving and other equipment
   e) the regulations of hours and conditions of work
   f) proper accommodation for passengers and seamen
   g) proper loading gear and inspection of same.
8. Commonwealth Bank of Deposit and Issue and Life and Fire Insurance Department, the management of each to be free from political influence.

9. Federal Patent Law, providing for simplifying and cheapening the registration of patents.

10. Uniform industrial legislation: alteration of Constitution to provide for same.[160]

---

[160] Australian Labor Party, <u>Second Commonwealth Political Labour Conference</u>. Official Report, 1902, pp.13-14.

Appendix 3 - Articles Of Alliance Between The Liberal Protectionist And The Labor Parties

Agreed to by ALP on 7 September and approved 14 September 1904

Conditions of Alliance

1. Each Party to retain its separate identity.
2. The Alliance to be for the life of this and the next Parliament.
3. Each to use its influence, individually and collectively with its organisations and supporters, and secure support for, and immunity from opposition to, members of either party, during the currency of the Alliance.
4. A joint election committee to consider contested seats, and to make recommendations to both parties.
5. Any member of the Parliament who agrees to this Alliance may, subject to the approval of both parties be admitted to this Alliance.

General Platform

1. The Conciliation and Arbitration Bill as nearly as possible in accordance with the original Bill as introduced by the Deakin Ministry, but any member is at liberty to adhere to his votes already given.
2. White Australia legislation - Maintaining existing acts in their integrity, and effectively supporting their intention by faithful administration.
3. The Navigation Bill - Report of Royal Commission to be expedited, and subject to this the Bill to provide for:
   a) Protection of Australian shipping from unfair competition.
   b) Registration of all coastal vessels.

c) Efficient manning of vessels.

d) Proper accommodation for passengers and seamen.

e) Proper loading gear and inspection of same.

4. Trade Marks Bill.

5. Fraudulent Marks Bill.

6. High Commissioner Bill - Selection of High Commissioner to be subject to prior consent of Parliament; the economising of existing State agencies, and full utilisation of Federal staff for the benefit of the States.

7. Electoral Act Amendment Bill.

8. Papua Bill

9. Anti-Trust legislation.

10. Tobacco monopoly - Appointment of present Select Committee as Royal Commission, with the addition of members of both Houses of Parliament.

11. Iron Bonus Bill - Every member to have freedom of action as to method of control.

12. Standing Committee on trade, commerce and agriculture.

13. Preferential trade to be discussed by joint parties at an early date

14. Legislation (including tariff legislation) shown to be necessary:

(1) To develop Australian Resources. (2) To preserve, encourage and benefit Australian industries, primary and secondary. (3) To secure fair conditions of labour for all engaged in every form of industrial enterprise and to advance their interests and wellbeing without distinction of class or social status. (4) As to any legislation arising under this paragraph only: - Any member of either party may as to any specific proposals: - (a) Agree with the members of his own party and be bound by their joint determination, or (b) Decide for himself how far the particular circumstances prove the necessity and the extent to which the proposal

should be carried. (5) A Royal Commission to be at once appointed to inquire into the necessity for tariff legislation; personnel to be approved by Parliament; commission to report in sufficient time to enable any desired legislation to be introduced next session.

15. Old Age Pensions on a basis fair and equitable to the several States and to individuals.
16. Quarantine legislation.
17. Either party may at any time submit to the other party any other subject for consideration with a view to joint action.[161]

---

[161] *Caucus Minutes*, September 6 1904.

Appendix 4 - Australian Labor Party Federal Platform 1908

General Platform - 1908

a. The cultivation of an Australian based sentiment, based upon the maintenance of racial purity, and the development in Australia of an enlightened and self-reliant community;

b. The securing of the full results of their industry to all producers by the collective ownership of monopolies, and the extension of the industrial and economic functions of the State and Municipality.

Fighting Platform

1. Maintenance of White Australia.
2. The New Protection.
3. Nationalisation of Monopolies.
4. Graduated tax on Unimproved Land Values.
5. Citizen Defence Force.
6. Commonwealth Bank
7. Restriction of Public Borrowing.
8. Navigation Laws.
9. Arbitration Act Amendment.

General Platform

1. Maintenance of a White Australia.
2. New Protection - Amendment of Constitution to ensure effective Federal Legislation for New Protection and Arbitration.
3. Nationalisation of Monopolies - if necessary, amendment of Constitution to provide for same.
4. Graduated Land Tax - Graduated tax on all estates over £5000 in value on an unimproved basis.

5. Citizen Defence Force, with compulsory military training and Australian owned and controlled Navy.

6. Commonwealth Bank of Issue, Deposit, Exchange and Reserve with non-political management.

7. Restriction of Public Borrowing.

8. Navigation laws to provide -

    a. For the protection of Australian shipping against unfair competition.

    b. Registration of all vessels engaged in the coastal trade.

    c. The efficient manning of vessels.

    d. The proper supply of life saving and other equipment.

    e. The regulation of hours and conditions of work.

    f. Proper accommodation for passengers and seamen.

    g. Proper loading gear and inspection of same.

    h. Compulsory insurance of crews by shipowners against accident or death.

9. Arbitration Act amendment to provide for preference to unionists and exclusion of the legal profession with provision for the inclusion of all State Government employees.

10. Old Age and Invalid Pensions.

11. General Insurance Department with non-political management.

12. Civil equality of Men and Women.

13. Naval and military expenditure to be allotted from proceeds of direct taxation.

14. Initiative and Referendum[162]

---

[162] Australian Labor Party, <u>Official Report of the Fourth Commonwealth Political Labour Conference</u>, Brisbane, July 7 1908, p.42.

7 BIBLIOGRAPHY

Newspapers

Queensland Worker, 3 February 1900.

Bulletin, 16 February 1901.

Advertiser, Adelaide, 1 September 1902

Daily Telegraph, 27 April 1904 (lead article)

Argus, 25 April 1904.

Primary Books, Manuscripts and Pamphlets

Papers of Alfred Deakin, National Library of Australia, Canberra. Watson to Deakin, 26 May 1904, MS 1540-16-62-s2-v.

Papers of Alfred Deakin, National Library of Australia, Canberra. Watson to Deakin, 30 May 1904, MS 1540-16-70-s1-e.

Papers of Alfred Deakin, National Library of Australia, Canberra. Watson to Deakin, 22 June 1905, MS 1540-16-392-s4-v.

Papers of Alfred Deakin, National Library of Australia, Canberra. Watson to Deakin, 28 June 1905, MS 1540-16-420-v.

Papers of Alfred Deakin, National Library of Australia, Canberra. Watson to Deakin, 5 July 1905, MS 1540-16-392-s4-v

Papers of Alfred Deakin, National Library of Australia, Canberra. Watson to Deakin, 22 June 1905, MS 1540-16-392-s4-v.

Papers of John Christian Watson, National Library of Australia, Canberra. Watson to Caucus, MS 451, Series 1 correspondence, 1903-1941

Papers of Alfred Deakin, National Library of Australia, Canberra. Watson to Deakin, 17 December 1906, MS 1540-15-656-s1-v.

Papers of Alfred Deakin, National Library of Australia, Canberra, Canberra. Watson to Deakin, 17 December 1906, ms 1540-15-656-sl-v.

Papers of Alfred Deakin, National Library of Australia, Canberra. Deakin to Watson, 20 December 1906, MS 1540-15-665-v.

Papers of John Christian Watson, National Library of Australia, Canberra. J.C Watson to Deakin, 27 December 1906, MS 451, Series 1 correspondence, 1903-1941. 158

Papers of Alfred Deakin, National Library of Australia, Canberra. Deakin to Watson, 20 December 1906, MS 1540-15-665-v.

Papers of Alfred Deakin, National Library of Australia, Canberra. Watson to Deakin, 27 December 1906, MS 1540-15-671-s2-v.

Papers of Alfred Deakin, National Library of Australia, Canberra. Watson to Deakin, 24 June 1908, MS 1540-15-824-v.

Papers of Alfred Deakin, National Library of Australia, Canberra. Deakin to Watson, undated correspondence 1909, MS 1540-16-595-s1-v.

Government Publications

C.P.D., Vol. 1, 22 May 1901, p.763.

C.P.D., Vol. V, 6 September 1901, p.4822.

C.P.D., Vol. V, 9 October 1901, pp.5848-53.

C.P.D., Vol. IX, 9 April 1902, p.11492.

C.P.D., Vol. XIV, 14 July 1903, pp.2044-5.

C.P.D., Vol. XIV, 21 July 1903, pp.2313-20.

C.P.D., Vol. XIV, 15 July 1903, p.2106.

C.P.D., Vol. XV, 4 August 1903, p.3034.

C.P.D., Vol. XV, 5 August 1903, pp.3102-3.

C.P.D., Vol. XV, 6 August 1903, pp.3206-7.

C.P.D., Vol. XVI, 8 September 1903, pp.4751-2.

C.P.D., Vol. XVIII, 17 March 1904, p.649.

C.P.D., Vol. XIX, 14 April 1904, p.947.

C.P.D., Vol. XVIII, 19 April 1904, p.1043.

C.P.D., Vol. XIX, 21 April 1904, pp.1242-3.

C.P.D Vol. XIX, 21 April 1904, pp.1248-1250,

C.P.D., Vol. XIX, 19 May 1904, pp.1296-7.

C.P.D., Vol. XIX, 31 May 1904, p.1676.

C.P.D., Vol. XXI, I 1 August 1904, p.4155.

C.P.D., Vol. XXI, 17 August 1904, p.4264.

C.P.D., Vol. XXI, 7 September 1904, p.4343.

C.P.D., Vol. XXV, 29 June 1905, p.60.

C.P.D., Vol. XXV, 10 August 1905, p.812.

C.P.D., Vol. XXVI, 24 August 1905, p.1436

C.P.D., Vol. XXVII, 28 September 1905, p.2893.

C.P.D., Vol. XXX, 20 December 1905, p.7456.

C.P.D., Vol. XXXIII, 16 August 1906, p.2894.

C.P.D., Vol. XXXV, 4 October 1906, p.6041.

C.P.D., Vol. XLIV, 19 March 1908, pp.9301-9351.

C.P.D., Vol. XLV, 3 April 1908, p.10,132;

C.P.D., Vol. XLV, 9 April 1908, p.10,406.

C.P.D., Vol. XLVI, 26 May 1908, p.11,421.

C.P.D., Vol. XLVI, 3 June 1908, pp.11933-4.

C.P.D., Vol. XLVIII, 10 November 1908, p.2140.

C.P.D., Vol. XLVIII, 10 December 1908, p.3087.

C.P.D., Vol. XLIX, 27 May 1909, p.126.

C.P.D., Vol. XLIX., 28 May 1909, pp.174-5.

C.P.D., Vol. L, 29 July 1909, p.1759.

New Protection - Memorandum relating to the proposed Amendment of the Constitution, <u>Commonwealth Parliamentary Papers</u>, 1908, Vol ii.

<u>ALP Federal Conference Records</u>

Australian Labor Party, <u>Second Commonwealth Political Labour Conference. Official Report</u>, 1902.

Australian Labor Party. <u>Third Commonwealth Political Labour Conference</u>. Melbourne, July 1905.

<u>Fourth Commonwealth Political Labour Conference</u>, Brisbane, July, 1908.

<u>ALP Federal Caucus Minutes</u>

Caucus Minutes, 31 July 1901.

Caucus Minutes, April 23, 1904

Caucus Minutes, May 17, 1904.

Caucus Minutes, May 17, 1904.

Caucus Minutes, May 25, 1904.

Caucus Minutes, May 26, 1904.

Caucus Minutes, September 6 1904.

Caucus Minutes, 29 June 1905.

Caucus Minutes, 5 July 1905.

Caucus Minutes, 5 July 1905.

Caucus Minutes, July 27 1905.

Caucus Minutes, February 19, 1907.

Caucus Minutes, October 30, 1907.

Caucus Minutes, October 30, 1907.

Caucus Minutes, 14 April 1908.

Caucus Minutes, 14 April 1908.

Caucus Minutes, 4 November 1908.

Caucus Minutes, 10 November 1908.

Books

Crisp, L.F., (1955) The Australian Federal Labour Party 1901-1951. Longmans, Green and Co. Ltd, Melbourne, Australia.

Faulkner, J. & MacIntyre, S., (2001) True Believer. The Story of the Federal Parliamentary Labor Party. Allen & Unwin, Australia.

Fitzhardinge, L., (1964) William Morris Hughes Volume 1: That fiery little particle 1862 -1914. Angus and Robertson, Sydney.

La Nauze, J. A., (1979) Alfred Deakin: A Biography. Melbourne University Press.

La Nauze, J.A., (1965) Alfred Deakin. MUP, Melbourne.

McKinlay. B., (1981) <u>The ALP: A short History of the Australian Labor Party</u>. Heinemann Publishers, Australia.

McMullin, R., (1991) <u>The Light on the Hill: The Australian Labor Party 1891-1991</u>. Oxford University Press Australia.

McMullin, R., (2004) <u>So Monstrous a Travesty: Chris Watson and the Words first national Labor government.</u> Scribe Publications Pty Ltd, Melbourne, Australia.

Palmer, N., (1931) <u>Henry Bourne Higgins</u>. Harrap Publishers, London.

Sawer, G., (1956) Australian Federal Politics and Law 1901-1929. Melbourne University Press.

Weller, P. (1975) <u>Caucus Minutes 1901 - 1949. Minutes of the meetings of the Federal Parliamentary Labor Pany. Volume 1-1901-1917</u>. Melbourne University Press.

ABOUT THE AUTHOR

Dr John McSwiney holds degrees in Social Science (Politics/Economics) and Law, he has a Masters of Arts (Politics) and a Doctorate of Philosophy from Monash University. John joined the Labor Party when he was 18 and won preselection for the Federal seat of Isaacs when he was 24 contesting the seat as part of Paul Keating's team at the 1993 Federal election. John has had careers in politics, law, government and international business. His roles have included being a Barrister and Solicitor of the Supreme Court of Victoria; the Director International Education, VCAA; CEO Haileybury International School, China; and Director, Technical Training (Eng.) Royal Australian Navy.

99